Margaret E. Shepherd
208 S. Washington
Wilmington, IL 60481

W9-CHN-647

UP FROM GRIEF

Bernadine Kreis and Alice Pattie

UP FROM GRIEF

Patterns of Recovery

The Seabury Press · New York

1982
The Seabury Press
815 Second Avenue
New York, N.Y. 10017

Copyright © 1969 by Bernadine Kreis and Alice Pattie
Library of Congress Catalog Card Number: 69:13542
ISBN: 0-8164-2364-4
Design by NANCY DALE MULDOON

Printed in the United States of America

All rights reserved. No part of this book may be used
or reproduced in any manner whatsoever without written
permission from the publisher, except in the case of
brief quotations embodied in critical
articles and reviews.

Second paperback printing

To Kay and John

PUBLISHER'S NOTE

Up from grief has been written to help those who are in grief, those who need to understand grief in order to help a relative or friend, and those who work with the grief-stricken.

Mrs. Kreis has done the actual writing, but both she and Mrs. Pattie, working as a team, conducted the research, shared in doing the five hundred interviews, evaluated the findings, and planned the book as a whole. The names of the persons interviewed have, of course, been changed.

CONTENTS

UP FROM GRIEF

Chapter One

GRIEF IS REAL

THE loss of my mother, my husband, and my father in quick succession taught me a great deal about grief. One of the most important lessons was the inestimable value of understanding friends.

Later, in talking with anyone who had a death in his family, I realized that whether the loss was a wife, husband, child, sibling, or parent, something went wrong in the way he was treated by his family and friends, his doctor and his minister. Some need was not met which made the grief harder to bear, harder to accept, and harder to recover from than one might think necessary.

Why should this be so? Strangely enough, inherent in grief there is hope, but it is beyond reach unless there is an understanding that grief is more than a word, that grief is real. The doctors say that grief is an illness called "reactive-depression," which moves through three predictable stages: shock, suffering, slow recovery. The goal is to have the period of recovery a healthy one.

Let us look at grief. If you have known it, you will remember. If you haven't: Imagine yourself suddenly alone in an alien world. Your body is weary, your emotions raw. Your heartache is a real physical ache and you are sure your life is destroyed. You do not know how to think, how to stop feeling, how to start feeling, where to go, where not to go, what to do, what not to do. Your emotions are a mixture of childish anger that "this should happen to me" and a mature awareness that the one you loved is gone. And yet paradoxically, for a while you do not believe he is really dead. You feel trapped, betrayed, and frightened. You feel guilt, anger, self-pity, and you long to share all these contradictory feelings with someone who understands, but you are afraid. All the conflicting emotions sink deep inside you. You wonder if you are going insane because you do not know if anyone else ever felt as you feel. Then you, like your friends, play the game called "Count your blessings." It is a hide-and-seek game. You hide your real feelings and seek approval from your friends by your strength in accepting grief with such good grace.

The key word in the foregoing description of grief is "afraid." All too often grievers are afraid to confide their real feelings to others, and all too often afraid to admit their real feelings to themselves.

There is an unwritten law that grief is a sad side of life, to be lived through without a real understanding of its patterns. And yet when we know the facts about any other aspect of life, even before we experience it, our anxiety is lessened, our sense of purpose strengthened. Knowledge cannot erase the emotions accompanying grief, but knowledge can help us guide ourselves and each other toward recovery.

How did I get to talk to people about grief? It all started when Alice Pattie and I were having dinner one evening, two lonely widows sharing a check. At first we just talked casually about grief, but not for long. Soon we were excited and stimulated, exchanging experiences and tossing ideas back and forth, forgetting to be "careful"—airing our mistakes and our hurts and our singular lack of specific knowledge. The relief and release we felt was gigantic. We had one strong bond: grief. We admitted our own lack of preparation for grief and the multitudinous words of bewildering rather than comforting advice tossed at us; the awkwardness of our well-intentioned families and friends, as unprepared to help in grief as we were unprepared to grieve. As widows we knew we had lost our social status completely, and we wondered if we were unique, which seemed unlikely since we were from different backgrounds, different professions, and different religions. We discussed the vast loneliness of grief and how much of that loneliness was imposed by others. We decided to read as many books "on grief" as we could find. We found very few that offered any practical advice. But hidden amid the dreary texts, we did find explanations of the three stages of grief. We wondered why we were not told there were such stages. We decided to talk with other grievers, their families and friends. Frankly, we were shy of starting, afraid we would be rebuffed or considered indelicate or intrusive. Instead, we found most people eager to talk, eager to share, and we soon learned that no one had really been prepared because no one knew what to expect, and no one knew what was "normal." Most people confessed they felt awkward with a griever. Afraid of saying the wrong words, doing the wrong things. They were afraid to be with a griever and afraid to stay away.

We decided to do our own small survey on "grief." But before we were through, by dividing our interviews, we had talked with five hundred grievers, their families, friends, and the pros who work closely with grievers: doctors, psychologists, lawyers, ministers—even a hypnotist and a plastic surgeon. Without exception, the professionals felt that a friend's involvement with a griever is essential to his recovery and that any drastic change in his way of life should be tackled only after the first stage of grief is over. Ministers of all denominations believe faith sustains but cannot erase the valid sorrow concomitant with losing a loved one. In studying the results of our survey we found that without exception all grievers were fascinated by the idea that grief did indeed have a pattern, no matter how nebulous. We tried to evaluate what is done to help the griever and what he does to help himself, hoping to find the down-to-earth, practical answers for today's living.

Within these pages you will meet many people, all kinds of people, the professionals who deal with grief constantly, the people in grief, and those who are recovering from it. You won't be exactly like any of them, but you may be something of all of them. No one can promise you a surcease from your suffering, but if you have lost a loved one, you will understand the patterns of grief far better, you will learn to recognize what stage of grief you are in, and you will find ways to search for new meanings in life which can lead to your recovery. If you are a friend or relative of a griever, you will feel less inhibited and therefore more spontaneous and helpful in your actions toward the grief-stricken.

In our society we are supposed to be a strong and courageous people and we urge grievers to be strong and courageous even at a time when it is unhealthy to avoid the normal suffering and heartache.

Why shouldn't we be allowed grief? Why do we consider emotion a weakness? At best, grief is a lonely state. No one can change that. But it is long past time to take a new look at grief and its aftermath of loneliness and heartbreak.

At present, a griever is left pretty much to his own devices. But why should we continue such malpractice?

Certainly it is in our own interest to change a situation we ourselves will face again and again throughout our lives. And why does a griever accept this neglect without protest? Why is he so submissive? Probably because when death strikes close he is too shocked to protest, then he is suffering too much to protest, and by the time he has regained some measure of equilibrium, he has conformed to a society which urges him to "carry on," "chin-up," "keep busy," etc., and he has accepted a false axiom that sorrow carries a stigma and must be overcome—but fast—because, "There is no other way . . ."

There are better ways and we owe it to ourselves to find them, and that is what this book is all about: a new look at grief. A deeper look. The world is full of widows and widowers and other mourners—has been, and always will be.

When we die, someone survives and feels a sense of loss. It happens every second of every hour of every day. And yet we have fallen into a dangerous pattern of avoiding grief, of treating it as a necessary evil, of reacting mechanically. When someone dies, there are things to do and we do them. But most of the time in so doing are we really facing grief? Are we really offering help to the grievers? Or are we only going through a series of motions, not *emotions*, doing what is expected of us, just that and no more? Grief does not fit into our way of life, therefore neither does the griever —except for a short period.

Modern life has no time for death. Death must of necessity be handled quickly, and be as quickly forgotten. But grief remains, and the puzzle is this: How to accept the breakup of family unity, and function amid the fast pace and the high pressure of life today so that grief does not destroy the survivors.

Who are the survivors? As soon as we are born, we are survivors. But we do not grieve for our ancestors because they have been long dead and we never knew them. In that context, death is not frightening. But when it comes close, it *is* frightening.

We are all survivors in this world simply because we are alive. We have goals, ambitions, and dreams. We eat, sleep, work, love, question, doubt, think, and feel. We have status in our society—we belong. But during our lifetime, we will lose many people we love. Friends, neighbors, relatives, perhaps a child—and in marriage, if we live long enough, a mate. Again and again we will be the survivor—the griever—but a different kind of griever, no longer in the abstract, theoretical sense. Suddenly but inexorably the safety of "we" becomes the isolation of "you," for now you are the suffering survivor. At this point society finds you a burden, even an embarrassment, because in this land death has become a taboo, and since the suffering survivor reminds us of death, as soon as you grieve you become an integral part of that taboo. Lost in our own fears, we turn away from you at a time when you need us the most.

Early grief is an illness which can be helped or impeded by those in contact with the grieving. Unfortunately, friends and family are apt to impede your recovery. Like most of us you come to grief unprepared, and once in it, you face it alone. We want to help you but we just do not know how. We go to a funeral or a memorial service. We pay a condolence call or we write a letter of sympathy. We may even see you once or twice, but we do not know what to say and we do not know what to do. So we go back into our own lives and you are left alone. We assure ourselves it is the "best way," but what we are not saying is that it is the best and easiest way for *us*. Oh, we rationalize our actions on the basis that "You will be all right. Time will heal . . ." But if you survive someone, someone very near and dear to you, you are immune to shallow words of comfort and hackneyed phrases; they just will not do. And what is more important, the shallow response only intensifies that feeling of "aloneness." We say: "By nature man is not a loner. He belongs with his group." But in grief you are forced to be alone. It is a role you find untenable and destructive. Your isolation is torture, augmenting your grief.

Of course part of the problem comes from the breakdown of family life. America is on the move. Young couples settle in small quarters away from home, children go out on their own at an earlier age, friends scatter. And all too often when grief-stricken, you are left alone to work through your grief in the best way you can. This is a strange phenomenon, since early grief is akin to a manic-depressive state. How, then, can you "cure" yourself?

On what basis would we expect any other ill person to cure himself? Little wonder that the grievers often make premature decisions: remarry out of desperation instead of love or withdraw into a partial suicide.

The society in which we live seems to be in desperate need of a re-evaluation and re-education on how to meet death. The majority of people are not prepared for it, and when it comes, they do not know how to face it, for themselves, for members of their families and their friends.

Consider: If you are an alcoholic, juvenile delinquent, an unmarried mother, an abandoned baby, or just getting old, society is there to cushion your problem. You can get help. But if you are in grief you soon discover that not only are you on your own in your trouble, but that few people really know *how* to help you.

In the chapters that follow, the isolated *you*, the griever, will find some explanation of your aching heart, disoriented life, sense of hopelessness and helplessness, and your terrifying restlessness. There will be reassurance that what you feel, others have felt; that what you suffer, others have suffered; that what you deny, others have denied; that your sense of guilt is not unusual, not shameful, but very normal.

As you read through these interviews with the grievers, and the ideas gathered from doctors, psychologists, and ministers, new doors will open and a fresh understanding will evolve so that you will be assisted and aided through the three stages of grief rather than impeded and abandoned. In reviewing this material, you will find yourself agreeing with one point of view, disagreeing with another. At times you may not like what is said at all—or you may like it very much, indeed. In any event, you will have many questions. And is not that the over-all value in discussing this provocative subject of grief? To find ways in which man can face the fact of grief and help others to do so, with a new depth of understanding. Therefore, if this material stimulates discussions, questions, and even some strong reactions, it will have served a most useful purpose.

If you prepare, think, plan to accept grief as an integral part of life, perhaps you can help reverse the dangerous trend of avoiding grief, which leaves you feeling that you are beyond solace and understanding when you need it the most.

Chapter Two

FIRST STAGE:
SHOCK

There are three stages of grief: shock, suffering, re-covery. This progression occurs in all kinds of grief. The duration of each stages differs with the nature of the grief, the character of the griever, and the depth of deprivation caused by the loss of another human being from the griever's life.

Even the news of the death of a casual acquaintance brings us to a standstill. "Oh, no," we'll say, caught for a moment by shocked dismay. "How did it happen? —When?"

The complexity of the three stages of grief is not in the intensity with which it hits the individual, nor with the duration of each stage, since neither can be measured accurately. No, the complexity is in the intricate pat-

tern of behavior in which a griever goes into shock, pro-
gresses into suffering, regresses back into shock, pro-
gresses back into suffering. Until the balance of recovery is stabilized, his moods swing unpredictably from
one stage to another—a terrifying situation for him and
for those who really want to help him.

In shock there is a chasm between the griever's logical thinking and his emotions. "Shock" is a generic
term covering a wide spectrum of conflicting emotions,
which are beyond analysis or logical thinking on the
part of the griever. As he tosses between these conflicting emotions, the griever may become trapped,
rendering him incapable of moving toward recovery.
Usually early grief is the only time in which he is still
surrounded by family and friends and forgiven any er-
ratic behavior. In most cultures, the griever is allowed
anywhere from one week to one month of shock. If
only more grievers could express their true feelings
and reactions then, the emotional release would ease
what is to come.

A frantic escape from shock is dangerous and eventually takes root in chronic depression. A griever may
try to cope with the separation of logic and emotion
by ignoring the grief that has caused his dilemma and
act out his life almost as if nothing had happened. "Escape from reality" the psychologists call it. He may col-
lapse, unable to function at all, which is an escape from
reality too. He may withdraw into a shell of silence to
hide his negative feelings of guilt, anger, self-pity and

frustration, or he may give way to his grief with periods of wild weeping mixed with periods of rigid control as he forces himself to mingle with family and friends.

But shock lacks rationality, and that is the most positive ingredient of grief. Therefore, if he can accept shock as inevitably complicated and frightening, he is facing reality. But if he is tossed into grief without preparation or knowledge of its patterns, and all too often supported by people who do not understand grief any better than he, the griever impedes his recovery.

What should he do? How should he act? He should act the way he feels with as much honesty as he can muster. He should, I should, and you should.

Don't try to cope with shock. Let it be. One day I was sitting on the beach, pretending to read, and a couple came over to talk with me. "I don't think you are doing the right thing," Leonard said. "One of my partners just died about the same time your husband, Kay, did. No more than two weeks ago, and his wife hasn't been alone at all. Her house is full constantly. Parties every night. She entertains lavishly and she is just great." His wife nodded, adding, "It's wrong for you to sit here and read or stare at the ocean. Why don't you entertain? Give a cocktail party?"

I felt guilty—why couldn't I do that? "Thank you for telling me about her," I said.

Weeks passed, and I began to join others on the beach. "By the way, how is your friend?" I asked Leonard. "You know, the one who entertained—lavishly . . ."

"Poor thing," he said. "She's had a breakdown. Nurses around the clock. No visitors allowed—and she was doing so well . . ."

"I'm so sorry," I said, but I was thinking, "Was she doing too well, too soon?"

Shock is nature's way of protecting you for the future. If you feel an obligation to perform nobly, by all means do it, but pretending to others is far different from pretending to yourself.

For no matter how you act, you will feel pulled in two opposite directions. You will feel restless and too weary to move; you will feel hatred and need love; you will feel alienated and need sympathy; you will feel mute and need communication; you will feel isolated and need companionship; you will feel half-dead, half-alive; you will feel nothing and too much; you will feel betrayed and abandoned—unloved, unloving, and unlovable. You will feel as guilty as a murderer and as martyred as a saint. At times your awareness will be acute, but clear thinking will be an illusion. All these feelings disconnect you from yourself and your environment, yet it is then you need people desperately to remind you that the world still exists, you still exist, an important person in your own milieu, wanted and loved for your own sake. And yet, surrounded by family and friends, funeral preparations and all the realities of death—you will deny death even as you discuss it.

This is not madness nor is it abnormal. Love does not die that quickly; it cannot be chopped down like a tree. I have never before heard anyone say this in just so many words: "Love cannot accept a death quickly." And if all grievers knew this to be a truth, they would suffer less, berate themselves less, and discuss it openly instead of hiding the knowledge as if it were a shameful secret.

The night of my husband's funeral, I remember how I cringed when a friend said: "I had lunch with Kay two weeks ago. I can't believe he's gone."

I closed my eyes trying to erase those words, and all at once *I saw Kay standing just inside the front door, looking as he always had coming home from work. He smiled and I ran into his outstretched arms as I always had and leaned against his chest.* I opened my eyes, the image was gone. I closed my eyes and the image returned again and again—day after day—week after week. I did not understand why I always saw re-enacted the very same moment of our life together. That one fleeting moment. Until months later, when I talked with a psychologist. I was disturbed, not by the recurring image which was so comforting, but because I just could not understand its meaning.

"It has several meanings, rather than one," the psychologist said. "You could call it a shock-absorber. It was your way of alleviating your grief. Too, it was a normal reaction to the death of a beloved and vital figure in your life. We don't stop loving someone at the precise instant he stops breathing. Your life was geared to his. Death came quickly, but the motion of your life together carried you forward on its own momentum as if he still lived."

"But why don't I get other happy images—why only this one?"

"An unconscious hope that he'll come back as he did every evening."

After finally confiding in someone, I was free to think about it and talk about it to other grievers. Each one had a comparable story to mine. Not the image necessarily, but a disbelief and a false hope. "Every time I phone my father," a college student told me after his mother died, "I expect to hear my mother's voice."

"I awaken several times every night, sure I hear Johnny crying," said a bereaved mother, "and I'm up and into his room before I remember . . ."

So it goes in early grief. There is no right or wrong to it. We feel too much or we cannot feel at all. We move from one emotion to another or we bog down with one emotion overriding all others. Gerald was a quiet, gentle man up to the moment a doctor told him his wife had died from injuries in an automobile accident. "I never felt so Goddamned mad," he said. "I just hauled off and punched him in the jaw."

When you grieve, try not to feel bitter when you lose the friendship of a few persons who are not grief-oriented. If they have visited you or called once or twice and then made the mistake of waiting for you to return either the visit or the call, they just do not realize that you have lost your initiative. How I wish everyone would learn the enormous effort it takes a new griever just to exist. There are always a few people who stand on ceremony. Your good friends take the initiative for as long as you lack it. They realize that you want them but cannot reach for them.

Anger in early grief often distorts the truth. One mother, whose daughter was thrown by a horse and killed, repeated over and over, "What did I do wrong?" That was self-condemnation, a twisted sense of guilt that grievers know all too well.

I remember flailing myself endlessly with questions which began with "If." "If I had chosen a different surgeon . . . If I had refused to let them operate at all . . . If . . . If . . ." What was I really saying? I was really saying that I should have been powerful enough to save my husband's life!

Grief's anger is irrational, born of frustration, and often acted out in a curious kind of rebellion. Elizabeth's husband was a minister. On Christmas Eve he had gone to buy her Christmas present and died in the department store. At the memorial service, Elizabeth wore a red hat. "Kenneth loved that hat," she had explained. "Besides, he didn't believe in black for mourning. . . ."

After calmer reflection Elizabeth realized she had worn the hat in rebellion against the congregation's expectation that she would be strong, supremely controlled, and ready to comfort them in their loss of a minister when, in fact, she grieved, not for the congregation or the minister, but for the man. Hers was a typical example of a tendency in early grief to offer one reason for a thought or an action, unaware that you mean another. She yearned for the Tender Loving Care children thrive on, since everyone in early grief is much like a child, and no adult is ever so self-sufficient that he is beyond the need of another human being's help.

As I point out these peculiarities of early grief, it might seem strange to someone who has never suffered the loss of a loved one, and it might seem like a gross exaggeration to those who have seen someone take a death very well. But I am not discussing what you see or think you see. I am discussing what you don't see and what all too often happens and is deeply hidden from the world—and worst of all, from the griever himself.

Betty's mother and father were killed in an automobile accident. Unprepared for such an event, they did not own a burial plot, and Betty, at sixteen years of age, decided against cremation. Her parents' bodies were laid in what she described as "receiving vaults." "I thought I was as miserable as anyone could get," she said. "But a year later there was another service—a proper burial—and I sure found out the difference between misery mixed with shock and plain downright misery. The first time the whole situation was unreal, like a nightmare. I had no such illusion for the second service. My God, it was far worse."

The necessity for shock in early grief can be compared to someone in great pain who "passes out." It is nature's way of protecting him from unbearable pain. After a death, the survivor "passes out" until he is ready to face the fact that a loved one is dead. That is why we cannot predict how long shock will last—a week, a month, a year. And that is why any loving support and real understanding from family and friends is so beneficial in aiding the griever's recovery.

It lessens his aloneness. Aloneness is quite different from loneliness. Thomas Wolfe said, "Loneliness is the central and inevitable fact of human existence." But while great loneliness exists in grief, it is not a synonym for grief. The grief-stricken are lonely, but the lonely are not necessarily grief-stricken. Each is tinged with the other but they are not interchangeable. Aloneness in grief is the loss of someone important to you and to whom you were important.

Last week I had dinner with a widower. He and his wife traveled extensively throughout their married life.

"I'm taking the month of August off," he said.

"What are your plans? Are you going abroad?"

"No—I haven't the faintest desire to go anywhere," he replied.

Now here is a charming man who never spends one evening at home—nor eats one meal at home unless he is entertaining friends. Living in New York City, he escorts one lady or another to Broadway shows, the opera, concerts, ballet. He accepts every invitation to dinner parties and cocktail parties galore. On the week-ends he visits friends in suburbia. So he is certainly not antisocial. Why then no vacation plans?

I did not venture a guess to him, but I have one. Al-though his wife died almost two years ago, I feel his overactive social life is an escape from aloneness. He senses that a trip by himself would reveal a truth he is not ready to face yet. He does not have one person to whom he is more important than anyone else.

Let us never belittle our need to feel important. The psychologists call it psychic-income.

I have mentioned the anger in early grief; the dis-belief in accepting death; the rebellion against what is expected of the griever; the irrational thinking which can sound reasonable; the guilt which is the self-con-demnation for a death; the overpowering weariness coupled with a constant restlessness; the aloneness which plagues the griever far more than loneliness. But I have not mentioned the lack of concentration that goes hand in hand with early grief.

I remember one of my sons visiting me soon after my husband's death. I had spent a distraught night wandering from one room to the other as if I were hopelessly lost in a dense forest. I remember my feeling of alienation from him because he tried to make conver-sation as if he were a casual acquaintance. Since then I have learned that the way relatives and friends treat a person who is bereaved is not determined as much by the relationship which exists between them as it is by their own personal attitude toward death.

That night, I did not know my son was uneasy in the apartment, still so full of reminders of his father. I did not know he was uneasy with me because he felt I had changed into an elusive personality—unfamiliar, therefore frightening. "Did you hear me?" he'd ask. "You're not listening to one word I say!"

"Oh yes, I am," I would pretend, trying to recall, if not his exact words, at least what he was talking about. Sometimes I would remember, but it was a horrendous visit for both of us. I felt so lost, so alone, so afraid. I wanted his reassurance that he had confidence in me— loved me. I wanted him to hold my hand so I would not float away. But at the same time he needed strength from me. He needed to feel that life would go on without his father. He needed what I could not give him and I needed what he could not give me. The tragedy was that neither of us could communicate our needs because we didn't know them ourselves. Luckily we were able to discuss it, not then but before the misunderstanding caused a permanent rift.

Shock brings with it still another obstacle to overcome. The physical manifestations, some of which we all know. The griever loses weight, eats little, sleeps fitfully, and looks drawn and haggard. But are we prepared for a tormenting chest pain? I was not. Are we prepared for a constant internal quivering that weakens our legs? I was not. Those are normal reactions; unfortunately no one tells us.

But once in shock can anyone penetrate your isolating numbness or can you help yourself?

Yes, if you are reminded you are in an abnormal situation—a reactive-depression caused by a normal fact of life: death. You may experience a little, some, or most of what I have described as the ingredients of shock. So be it. More than likely you will appear outwardly as your family and friends do in grief, not because you feel exactly as they feel, but because it is easier in shock to follow a prescribed pattern of behavior. How you react outwardly is far less important than how you treat yourself inwardly. Be kind to yourself. Forgive yourself any of those negative emotions like guilt, self-pity, or bitterness. One young man said his cousins and aunts were unavailable during his mother's terminal illness. The day of the funeral, as he left the grave-site, an aunt came over to him. "I know this is a bad time for you," she said. "But the diamond brooch your mother always wore—I'd love to have it. I wanted to ask before someone else did . . ." He stared at her, too angry to answer. But last week when he told me the story, he was still bitter although his mother had died six years ago.

Allow yourself tears, you are entitled to weep. Do not fear for your sanity if you cannot think clearly or reason rationally. It is not insanity, it is shock.

When we interviewed grievers, we found that each and every one began the interview by saying, "My family and all my friends were just marvelous." After a while I wondered: Is this universal? But when these grievers began to give details, a different, less perfect picture emerged. It would seem that family and friends do try, but they fall away too soon and those who remain, with some exceptions, flood the griever with advice. Even the fortunate few who have large doting families cannot escape the shock of a new grief or that feeling of being isolated in a crowd.

Try to find just one person in whom you can confide your innermost feelings and thoughts. Someone who will not sit in judgment; someone who will listen with understanding sympathy. If not within your family or friends perhaps your doctor, minister, or psychologist.

You have many immediate decisions to make and details to handle—so leave your future plans to the future. To those who offer advice about "What you should do," lend a passive ear. You are not ready for any major changes. You are ready only for loving acceptance that you are what you are—in shock. Just that and no more. Shock is—let it be.

Chapter Three

SECOND STAGE:
SUFFERING

THE long slow adjustment of living without someone you love is the second stage of grief—called suffering. I cannot begin to define suffering objectively because it is such a personal emotion and so much of your reaction depends upon the kind of person you are.

There are those who lack the ability to show emotion, but feel it deeply; and there are those who can live effectively only if they deny their distress; and there are those who have been so emotionally involved with a loved one that they lose their *raison d'être* when grief strikes and come to an emotional dead-end. These are grievers who for one reason or another cannot discharge the emotions which would help them through a normal cathartic grief. Not to confuse the

24

issue but to admit the wide range of suffering, I knew one woman who went to bed and stayed there, inconsolable for over six months, and then as if by magic returned to the mainstream of life in good spirits. You see, there is no right or wrong way to work through grief. There is the intricate task of finding your own way.

Hidden or exposed, the three stages of grief remain. The suffering stage of grief is the worst stage of all. Most people found that releasing despair by admitting it to themselves and others helped them through this horrendous experience. Am I saying that suffering is healthy? Yes, I am saying just that. I know it sounds preposterous, but when you lose someone you love, you are under violent stress. Death has swept a human being out of your life, never to return. The result is a helpless hopelessness. To those who express their suffering, the road to recovery seems a little easier. Any emotion expressed is a release of pressure whether the emotion is anger, love, or grief. Therefore, for our purpose we shall assume you want to express your emotions and share your experiences with others who have suffered—learn how they live with it, what mistakes they made, what helped them, and how they moved toward recovery.

You suffer in the shock stage too, but not as acutely because you have not had the experience of living with grief, only the prospect. Shock is a dreamlike state infused with suffering. Then as family and friends drift back into their own lives, you are left to face the future alone. At that point is it wise to withdraw into a dark tunnel of loneliness? The temptation beckons to withdraw completely. No longer dreamlike, the suffering becomes a sleepless nightmare; yet, despite the agony, it is nature's way of cleansing your wound. It is much like the rise and fall of waves hitting against the shore. There is the crash of an oncoming wave and the lull as it recedes. Suffering is like that. It comes and goes in waves of pain, then recedes only to return, deep and penetrating, but never constant.

Therefore, complete withdrawal only accentuates the crash of suffering, leaving you to brood through the lull instead of using it to talk with close, sympathetic friends.

I have stated again and again the importance of the role your friends and family can play during the shock of grief. Now I state unequivocally the importance of the role they can play during the stage of grief called suffering. Don't turn away from them. The more they understand, the more they include you in their lives, the more they convey by word and deed that you are a valuable person in your own right, you belong, you have roots, that when you are ready to move toward your future, they will help you find it—the greater your chance of recovery.

It isn't that you want to become a parasite feeding on other people's lives. The truth is that you move from shock to suffering. You are not ready to "be" yet. Beyond the empty look on your haggard face, there is an agonizing emotion ripping you apart. That is the second stage of grief—the full realization that you are grieving. Little wonder that you need more reassurance than you ever did before, more distractions and far more affection. If you get this support when you need it, your inner strength is free to confront suffering, work through it, and begin slowly but surely to find your own future.

Every griever has heard that "Time heals all wounds." Not always true, realistically or symbolically. People die of physical wounds and people become emotional cripples from a wound called "unresolved grief." Unresolved grief occurs when you cannot face some inner struggle, nor sublimate it in the first two stages of grief. An extreme example is the griever who leaves a child's room intact for years as if the child were still alive.

I did not know what held me in shock for too long a time. I know now. It was guilt. At one time or another, most grievers are caught by a negative emotion or a false notion that haunts them. The veil of sorrow is more impenetrable than any Iron Curtain. Perhaps it is the elusive quality of shock and suffering —so difficult to explain in words and even more difficult to live through.

The day of my husband's operation, our older son, Bob, the assistant conductor of the Pittsburgh Symphony Orchestra, met me at the hospital. But the doctor told Bob to take me home. "You'll be sitting here all day. It's a long operation. I'll call you when it's over. You should be able to see him about six o'clock." The doctor turned to me. "After the operation, even though he'll be drowsy for a few days, you can sit in his room and he'll enjoy seeing you each time he wakens."

"Good. That's what I want." Indeed that was what I wanted—to be there every time he opened his eyes.

At home our telephone rang all day. Friends. Bob talked for me. He told the switchboard operator to cut in on any call if the doctor was on the wire. We began to jump each time the phone rang. Finally it was the doctor. "As I suspected," he said. "A small tumor. They are doing a biopsy now. He is doing just fine! Get here about seven o'clock."

At the hospital, we waited and waited and waited. Seven, eight, nine, ten—the doctor appeared. "He's in the recovery room. Better go home. He won't be awake tonight. He's doing very well."

Wednesday: Bob and I went to the hospital. Kay was awake. He looked pale. Tubes ran from his chest into a glass container and I could see blood dripping into it. Another tube fed glucose into his arm. Kay asked us how *we* were and slept again. The nurse asked us to leave, since he would be sleeping most of the time.

We met the doctor in the corridor. "Sleep is good. I agree with the nurse. He is pretty doped up, you know. Come back about five."

"I have a concert," Bob said. "Is my dad doing well enough for me to fly to Pittsburgh just for tonight?"

"Of course."

"What did the biopsy show?" I asked.

"The beginning of a cancer," the doctor said. "They removed a portion of his lung to be on the safe side. I'm very pleased. All the surrounding area was normal and healthy."

Bob left for Pittsburgh. I went home and wrote a letter to Kay. The phone rang constantly. Why could I not distinguish one voice from another? Just as I was ready to leave for the hospital the phone rang again. It was Kay. "Darling, they say you had better not come up tonight—some tests or something. See you tomorrow, early? Love you."

Thursday: A long wait in the corridor before I could get in. Kay was awake and in great pain. I noticed the container on the floor was still bloody. The atmosphere was bustling as the nurse arranged a tray of tubes and ice. "You only have a few minutes—they'll be coming in any minute now—oh, nothing unusual— all routine."

I called the doctor. "Kay's in pain," he said. "We suspect a bleeding ulcer. I'm bringing in a specialist for consultation. I'll call you at home."

Kay called. "Darling, they are going to operate. I'm glad. The pain is pretty bad——" His voice trailed off.

"Kay, I love you." He did not answer. Two major operations in two days. I called my younger son, Peter, who was in the Air Force, stationed in Omaha, Nebraska, and Bob. "You'd better come home."

Wait . . . wait . . . wait . . . I had tried to protect my father from it all because my mother had died about one year before and he was still in grief, but now I had to bring him in to accept telephone calls. I could no longer talk to anyone. Six hours later the doctor called. "It was an ulcer. Kay's in the Intensive Care Ward. He came through with flying colors. Come right up."

The ward was full of patients. In the corner bed was Kay. Now there were tubes from his stomach, tubes from his chest, the glucose tube attached to his foot and an oxygen tent blowing steam around his head. Yet, he seemed alert. He pressed my hand through the oxygen tent. He didn't seem surprised to see Peter.

It was our anniversary. "Did you find the package I left for you?" Kay asked.

"Yes. I'll bring it tomorrow," I said. "We'll open it together."

"Marvelous idea." He sounded weak. "I'm glad you're all here. Yesterday I thought it was curtains for me and I was here alone——" He drowsed off before I could explain.

"We've turned the corner," said the doctor. "He'll be fine now."

For three more days we were allowed to see him in the Intensive Care Ward—five minutes in the morning, five minutes in the evening. Then he was moved back into a private room and the doctors had a conference at the foot of his bed.

"Are you pleased with our patient?" the doctor asked.

"More than pleased, I'm delighted," the surgeon said.

Kay squeezed my hand, and through the oxygen-tent material his hand felt very hot. Out in the corridor, the surgeon told Peter and Bob it was safe to go back to their jobs. "We're pumping your dad with vitamins. Tomorrow we start feeding. We've turned the corner—he'll be fine!"

Now I didn't believe anything the doctors said and I was angry at my sons as they kissed me goodbye and left. Could they not see something was wrong?

I sat watching Kay for a long time, but he did not wake up and they suggested I go home and sleep through the night as he would. It was one week since his first operation. Lack of sleep and the crumbs of food I had managed to swallow were beginning to have an effect on my body and spirit. "I must look better when Kay sees me tomorrow," I said, remembering the doctor's smiles and enthusiastic words. After all, they would not send Peter back to Omaha and Bob back to Pittsburgh unless they were sure everything was fine. But why was Kay's hand so hot and why was blood still draining from that tube? "I'm just tired," I told myself. The phone rang and rang . . . friends . . . business associates . . . their voices were like bees buzzing against my ear. I couldn't distinguish one from another. Angry now, I showered and dressed. Damn it, rules or no rules, I was going to sit in Kay's room as they had promised I could. The doorbell rang. It was our doctor. His expression was different. "Something has gone wrong," he said, holding my hand. "He's taken a turn for the worse——"

"Shall I call the boys?"

"Yes, you better."

Peter could not get a scheduled flight, so rather than wait, he decided to hitch an Air Force flight to Washington and then change to a commercial line. His wife, Suzi, would take the first scheduled flight from Omaha.

Bob was with me in a few hours. I had hurried to the hospital. I found Kay alone in the room, half out of the oxygen tent, half out of bed, straining against the tubes. He was terribly agitated. "I want to go home— now," he said over and over again. Nurses and attendants swooped in en masse and squeezed me out. Then, as two internes walked past, I heard one say, "I had to see that man. How is it possible with all the antibiotics we have used, he's dying?" I knew they meant Kay, but I refused to accept it. My legs were shaking so much I had to lean against the wall and inch back to Kay. Now he was quiet and his eyes were closed and from afar I knew I was being led away and into a taxi and I was home with Suzi, Peter, and Bob. Soon the doctor joined us. "He's in a coma. He may still——"

"What are his chances?" Bob asked. "Can he live?"

"There is a possibility—but not a probability." Gone was the cheerful smile, the cheerful word. He took me aside. "You're in bad shape. Swallow these."

"No. I must——" I swayed. "I must get to the hospital."

"You will." I swallowed the pills and just before I fell into a drugged sleep, I saw Suzi sitting close by and I realized how alone I had been through the days of false hope, false promises. Days spent in taxis, in the hospital corridors or waiting rooms, but hardly ever with Kay.

The doorbell awakened me. It was Peter and Bob. "He's gone," Peter said. "He never woke up—I stayed with him. I called, even yelled in his ear, because I wanted him to know he wasn't alone, but he never moved."

They stood watching me, waiting for my reaction, but I was thinking I had to get to Kay. The phone rang. It was the surgeon. "I'm so terribly sorry, we just do not know what went wrong. May we do an autopsy?"

"Will it hurt him?"

"No."

Again I was not to see Kay. "Well, I will be dead in a little while anyway," I promised. Aloud I said, "Cut-cut-cut-that's all they have done for seven days and now they are cutting again. My darling, oh, my darling . . ."

I sat with my knees against my chest and began to cry in that ugly anguish of grief and guilt. Not once had I been there when he awakened. I was convinced if he had seen me each time he opened his eyes he would have lived. You see? My normal despair was complicated by a false guilt which I couldn't accept as false until a year later when my dad was in the hospital after a heart attack.

I resolved that no one was going to keep me out of my father's room. This time I would be strong instead of passive. I refused to leave the hospital. I kept a vigil in the corridor right outside his room so I could hear when he was awake and reassure him that he was not alone.

Finally, the heart specialist, whom I had just met, came out of my dad's room, took me by the hand, and led me to an empty waiting room. "You and your father are both widowed, aren't you?"

"Yes."

"I hope my kids care as much about me as you do about your dad—but you are exhausted. Why don't you go home and rest and come back later."

"I can't," I said. Suddenly I found myself telling him about my husband. "I won't let it happen again!"

"Your father is on the critical list. Our main concern is keeping him alive. Don't you see we can't give a damn about you!" He placed an arm around my shoulders. "If they kept you out of your husband's room it was for the same reason. They were busy trying to save his life. You can't play God or doctor or nurse."

That night I called the surgeon who had operated on

Kay and asked him, "If I had refused to leave, if I had been there every time my husband awoke—could it have helped at all?"

"No, Mrs. Kreis. If a patient withstands an operation and is recuperating, then it does help to have the family there—but as it was, to put it bluntly, you were in the way. Besides, your husband was too ill to know."

If only I had called him months before, how much torture I could have saved myself. How much suffering I had heaped on already overburdened shoulders —mine.

As you vacillate between shock and suffering, you will hurt yourself far more than anyone else can ever hurt you. Anger against the doctor or the hospital for not saving the one you love; anger at God or Life for doing this to you; anger at those who offer advice you resent or resist; and under all the anger there is a huge open wound that medicine cannot heal; an empty space in your heart that no one else can fill.

What should you do with this anger? Call it by its proper name—GRIEF. That helps the most. It alleviates the suffering because grief is suffering, and disguising it into another emotion only bewilders you.

Watch children. They are wise in the ways of grief. A playmate moves away. A pet disappears. A toy breaks. They feel they "lose" mother to a new baby. What do they do with grief? They cry; they yell with the pain; but they suffer without one iota of disguise. They are not ashamed of their feelings. That helps.

Life prepares us for grief from the time we are children; so that by the time death comes, we have already experienced some of its suffering if only in small doses. Yet, somehow we lose the purity of facing grief when we are old enough to recognize that a precious human being is gone forever, at least in this world.

To suffer alone is better than trying to escape from it. But to share your suffering with each and every person you meet—don't! You lose too many friends that way. In shock you are expected to share your grief, as if it were real grief, which it is not; when you are suffering, you are expected to be recovering, which you are not. How all this misunderstanding about the patterns of grief came about I just do not know, but unless you are talking to another griever, the reactions expected of you are correlated to the community rather than to the griever. Most people think you are suffering when you are in shock, and think you are recovering when you are suffering. It is only when you have recovered that you belong to your group again. In the interim there is always someone who really understands and wants to help. Some one, perhaps two or three. My implication is this: For the community in which you live, you need to hide your real feelings. I know it sounds cruel if I suggest you go places, meet with friends, work, even play—when you are suffering. It sounds like a direct contradiction to other suggestions I have made about honesty. It is not a contradiction at all. Always be honest about yourself to yourself—and to your chosen confidants.

Since you need friends and relatives to save you from isolation and they need you to be cheerful and optimistic, you have little choice. I, and most of the grievers I interviewed, found that for a valid recovery, girding yourself each day to join the world as if you are cheerful and optimistic is of inestimable value. There is no magic formula that can cloak you with the joy of life, but a willingness to search for it is a good, even creative, first step. At times this involves accepting things as they are; at others, it means daring to change your way of life.

Not when you are in shock, and not when you are in that first agony of suffering, but as the days turn into weeks—however long it takes you to reach the moment of truth in which you realize that your grief is not going to disappear miraculously; that you may be scarred by the wound for a long, long time. When you realize you are alive, perhaps for a reason you do not understand, this is the moment to force yourself to begin to discover who you are now, what you want, where you belong, and what you want to do. A tall order. The answers come slowly through trial and error—with suffering.

Fundamentally, the search will begin with people in general and filter through them until you find the special friends with whom you have the freedom to communicate; the continuity of meeting often and a mutual exchange of interests.

A comparative stranger may become a close friend. Often it is far easier to be close to someone who never knew you before your grief. Old friends unwittingly wait for you to return to them as you were, which is unrealistic.

When Barbara was thirty, her mother died. She followed the advice usually given to people who live alone. She moved to a city, found a job, joined a club, and volunteered as a nurse's aide. Attractive, bright, and outgoing, she soon became popular, busy—and very bitter. She was rarely alone, but she lacked even one relationship with depth. She found a whirling social life barren; activities per se are not enough. She yearned for a few key relationships with whom she could share experiences and confidences.

Therefore, when you begin to "go out and do things," search for relationships which have real meaning. Search for the sensitive human being, the listener who responds with sincere warmth, but be prepared to reciprocate wholeheartedly. Thus do friendships flourish.

I am sorry that the world of the grievers has never been charted, even though it is inhabited by millions —always has been, always will be.

So it follows, as your suffering folds into despair, you have a choice—either sink with the despair or force yourself to rejoin the human race. The love you had for one, offer to others. At least try.

Please remember that the prerequisite for moving toward recovery is an integral part of every human being. Time is probably the most vital element in finding what to do—and when. Keep track of what stage of grief you are in, and do not condemn yourself if you move slowly from one stage to another or if you bog down in nostalgia or regret, even self-pity. Regression is not to be feared but expected.

There is no definite line of demarcation between the stages of grief. You drift from one stage to the other imperceptibly, but there is an undercurrent of strength protecting you and lifting you toward recovery.

Watch for your reactions to people and the advice offered. Take time; do not rush through any stage because, in so doing, you hamper your own progress if you push past where you really are.

Grief is like walking along a dark corridor with many doors that you can open—when you are ready. Some will be the wrong doors for you. But the very act of opening one after the other becomes a motivating force moving you forward. That is the beginning of recovery. A faltering step, but a step nonetheless.

Chapter Four

THIRD STAGE:
RECOVERY

THE third stage of grief is recovery. Like shock and suffering, it does not happen in a quick flash of insight. However, there are recognizable guideposts revealing the onset of recovery if you are on the alert and watch for their appearance.

Keep in mind that the dimension and length of each stage of grief depends upon your life-relationship with the one who died. If you have watched a lingering illness devour someone in slow deterioration, your grief will be shortened in gratitude that the suffering was snuffed out with life. Too, if the person who died was someone you loved, but was a person with whom you had had little contact for years because he had lived in another state or country, his death would touch you but not with the same anguish as if he had lived close by and were an integral part of your daily life.

There is no rule distinguishing the importance of one death from another. Generalities cannot be applied to grief. For instance, the death of an aged parent would not seem to evoke great grief, since one might assume he has lived a long and fruitful life. But suppose he was someone who depended on you; or suppose you depended on him; or suppose you lived within each other's orbit—then the grief would be deep. The same thing applies to a child's death. If he dies as an infant, one would expect a shortened grief, since your relationship had little time to become entrenched with a myriad of memories or shared experiences. Yet, to a young mother who carried that child for nine months and labored to give birth, a great sense of loss is possible.

People looking in on grief as bystanders cannot measure the intensity by a general rule. And you can not react as if any generality applies to you. What you feel—you feel! And only on what you feel can you react. Again we come face to face with inner honesty. The right to react to any death according to your own emotions.

In shock, the griever usually reacts within the mores of his community. But the disbelief and the numbness are there, whether hidden or exposed. In suffering, you begin to feel the loss, first in flashes of insight and then in prolonged reality. The pain turns from preoccupation about the one who died to anxiety about your own future.

As your thoughts become active, if only in anticipation of action, you are preparing to recover. Before I go any further let us examine the difference between actions in recovery as compared to actions in shock or suffering. In shock, your actions are mechanical. You do what you have to do. In suffering, your actions are forced by convention or by your own restlessness. But in recovery, your actions are by your own free choice.

When a griever forces himself to go to work, to visit with friends, or to take a trip, if it is not too early in grief, the repetition can induce recovery signs, since he may come to realize that he is needed in his work, wanted by his friends, distracted by his travels. But as long as he forces his actions, he is still in the suffering stage. To be ashamed of the stage of grief you are in is to deny your own nature and the fabric of grief that is yours.

One young widower insisted he had suffered his grief during his wife's long illness. He even talked enthusiastically of a girl he had just met. In the midst of all his positive protestations, he turned to me and asked one wistful question: "How long *does* this feeling of emptiness last?" I knew then that he was whistling in the dark; that the new girl he had mentioned was in his life too soon. That he will remarry, I have little doubt; but that he is far enough out of suffering to do so, I have great doubt.

When we define the three stages of grief, we define the routine of living for those who survive. The religious and the unreligious all suffer the grief that accompanies human separation. The painful burden of sorrow dissolves slowly, and out of the bleak suffering emerges a new kind of strength and wisdom. If you have kept a steady pace with your grief, you emerge with a surprising ability to balance the important against the unimportant, which means a new set of values. For once having tasted the finality of separation, small annoyances have little validity. To be more specific, you learn early in grief that you are very vulnerable and easily tossed upon a sea of hurts. You learn, slowly but surely, that you have the strength to shrug off an insensitive person. It no longer matters that much.

When some of my own family and friends withdrew into silence, ignoring me as if I, too, had died, I was deeply hurt. But with time, I learned to accept their actions with a new logic. If they were hurt by my passivity during shock, they did not understand grief. If they nursed some inadvertent slight during my suffering, they lacked compassion. And if they stubbornly held this silence—that was their problem, not mine. Logically, as a widow, perhaps I had less to offer them. So be it.

In grief, it is as if you are a lost soul wandering in the wilderness, sometimes idly, sometimes frantically. To find your way back is a constant challenge. I cherish those who never wavered in their support. I slough off those who withdrew.

A young woman in New York City related a bitterly amusing experience. The week after her mother died, she received two letters from relatives in California—they were husband and wife. The husband's letter said: "Now that you are alone, why don't you visit us for a few weeks. It would be such a good change for you. Just let us know how soon you can make it." How wonderful, she thought, I am so weary. She opened the wife's letter: "I do wish we could invite you to visit us," the wife wrote, "but we have a steady flow of guests. So sorry." The young griever's emotions shifted from hurt to anger, to perplexity. Didn't the husband and wife communicate with each other? Finally, she was amused. "I never had such acceptance and rejection at one and the same time," she said, smiling. She wrote a note of thanks for their condolences and never mentioned the visit.

"Did you get another invitation?" I asked.

"No. We'd been so close before they moved away, when I didn't hear from them again, I wrote the wife and asked if I had done anything to hurt her feelings. She wrote that I had not hurt her feelings, and if I ever did she would surely tell me."

"Then?"

"Complete silence. Sometime later I heard they had a death in the family, and I called long distance. The conversation was friendly enough. But they have remained silent ever since. So that's that. You know how it is when you grieve, you're not with it. That woman is nursing a grievance. Heaven knows what."

This is an extreme example of a silence that often descends on grievers, a baffling hurt because it is never explained. When you are tossed into grief and people you knew quite well just disappear "like that," you can choose between bitterness and compassion. When you choose *compassion*, you look at what you have and are grateful. There are loyal friends and relatives, and there are new friends.

At first, recovery is more philosophical than active. You toss ideas about, playing with one possibility after another, some wildly impractical, born of wishful thinking; but whatever their caliber, they represent a long hard look at the future.

Most grievers find that acting on those first tentative plans is dangerous, especially irreversible decisions like selling your house, moving away, or changing jobs. It is far wiser to mull over any idea for awhile until it can be thoroughly digested. You need to find the patience to wait out any irreversible decision until the desire for change becomes more than a capricious need to escape suffering and has a definitive purpose.

What about regression? Do grievers, moving toward recovery, regress into suffering? Always. Birthdays and anniversaries and holidays are particularly difficult. The lonely days and empty hours, which are inevitable in grief, bring a sudden lurch of longing—even despondency if there are too many of them.

One of my friend's sons was killed in the war—his body lost at sea. A few years later we were at a luncheon and someone showed pictures of skindivers. They were underwater shots. Quickly my friend jumped up and ran out of the room. I found her hunched in a chair, crying. "Oh, my God, those horrible pictures," she sobbed.

A song, a book, a place—almost anything can catapult you into the tunnel of despair. The most poignant regression comes if you face another death.

I remember standing at my father's burial, listening to, but not hearing, what the minister said. I touched my father's coffin in a last farewell, and as I turned to place roses on two other graves—my husband's and my mother's—I felt an overpowering fear, which made me quiver in its intensity. Not fear of dying. Just the knowledge that the ones who loved me, believed in me, and needed me most were all dead. Only one grave was empty—mine.

I remember the night before my mother died. I was in her room saying goodnight. "Who is here for dinner?" she asked.

"We all are."

"How wonderful," she said. I kissed her, not knowing it was for the last time.

I remembered the moment just before they took my husband to the operating room. We clung to each other.

"I'll be waiting. I love you," I said. "And, I love you," he said. "Take care."

That was our last conversation.

I remembered when my father had his heart attack.

He said to me, "Darling, I don't think I'll make it," and collapsed in my arms.

Who would be there for me? That was my fear as I listened and didn't hear what the minister said at my father's funeral. Self-pity? Yes, obviously. But also a frightening truth. Sooner or later every griever seems to fall into a darkened pool of self-pity. But it can be a creative force unless it continues unabated. What do I mean by "unabated"? A self-pity that bedevils you, crowding out every other emotion. Creative self-pity pulls you away from the hollow mind of grief toward a renewal of your identity as a human being who still lives.

The distant hill of recovery is man-made, built stone by stone by the griever and, if he is fortunate, with the aid and support of empathetic people watching his progress and helping when he grows too discouraged or too weary.

When he stumbles, even falls in his laborious way, he fights to survive, knowing that to stand still is to dwell in sorrow, to move forward, to live in hope. That a griever can never return to what he was, and knows it, is a sure guidepost of recovery. After a death there is in life no road at whose turning he and his loved one can meet again. A fact which leaves an indelible mark on his personality, his countenance, and his philosophy.

In comparison to the stages of shock and suffering, you will notice that I speak of recovery with a different emphasis on the roles of family and friends. Although recovery takes far longer unless friends and relatives have been supportive during your shock and suffering, their role decreases in activity with time, and the griever takes up the slack with his growing maturity and the knowledge that the challenge, the work, and the inner understanding come from within.

Have you ever watched a small child in a playground? At first he stays very close to his mother. She shows him how to use his sandbox toys, stands by as he tries the jungle gym, and then he moves in rhythm with the other children, doing as they do, but he glances toward his mother frequently to be sure she is near, and he returns to her side again and again to share the moment or to see her smile of approval. Should she leave, the joy of his play is instantly replaced by the fear of abandonment. Panic sets in. As he grows accustomed to the playground and other children, he is satisfied to know she is there and will not leave; or if it is a backyard, he is satisfied as long as he knows she is at home. He feels secure with less supervision—still needing the security but less in evidence.

The griever is like that small child who needs security, growing bolder if the security is solid and dependable until independence replaces dependence and the child reaches for mother only in time of hunger, fear, or to share pride in a new achievement. That kind of support is also the griever's need.

Now let us suppose you are a lone survivor or cannot confide in anyone easily—how then will you recover? It would help if you could find one person with whom you could share your real thoughts and feelings in order to clear the cluttered whirlpool of your mind. But if you cannot find anyone who will listen and understand or if there is something within you that demands silence, you will be forced to play two roles, the griever and the watchful supporter. Remember, at best a griever enters the world of grief alone, even those surrounded by loving friends and relatives. I know, I have been there. In that strange and frightening place of grief, every light and shadow is as alien to you as the landscape of Mars. You do not know the way, you make a thousand mistakes in direction. You move in a labyrinth of bleak corridors. You are not schizophrenic, but your life is split because part of you lives on while part of you wonders what to do with a huge piece of your future hopelessly dead. And you know you will carry it dead within your being for the rest of your life.

Let your wounds bleed, and your tears fall without restraint. Then begin to watch for snatches of hope. Cling to them as they come. Embroider them with humor, a sense of being challenged. Watch for a spark of spirit—the will to do, to be.

The nights will be long and tortuous. You will awaken hearing sobs. They will be your own. If you are widowed, you will awaken with an arm outstretched, reaching for the unreachable. All grievers know these things, in one way or another, for a long time. But if you watch yourself carefully, what eventually starts as a dim daydream of hope can be nursed into action. As you look forward, instead of backward, remember that Shakespeare said we are all actors. Try putting on a personality each morning as you do your clothes. Reason that if *you* do not like the way you look or act, and you will not, surely others will not either. Look around. There are so many unhappy people, perhaps you can offer them what you wish you had received. It is a reversal procedure—from looking inward to looking outward. At first it works better with strangers. A smile, a friendly exchange, then on to acquaintances, a lunch shared, conversation. All forced, all pretend. And one day the smile will be real, the interest in others deep, and your disciplined pretense becomes a reality, on and off, now and then, until you have forgiven Life for hurting you, and Death for taking someone whom you needed so much and who hadn't lived long enough.

At long last, almost all grievers come to believe they are alive for a specific unknown reason. Some call it a hunch; some call it God's Will; some call it Fate. Invariably it is a strong motivation leading the griever to work, each in his own way, toward recovery.

Chapter Five

THE GRIEVERS

Soon after the funeral-cousins and casual friends disperse; the griever is left to the smoke of his memories; the exploration of what happened; how he was involved; and what it all did to him as an individual.

To know and understand yourself is always difficult, but never so difficult as it is in grief—and never more important. Every death leaves its scars on the griever and part of a healthy recovery is in remembering. The mental re-enacting of your role before and after death leads you from what you were to what you are.

As I talked with grievers, I was struck by a recurring pattern. Whether the conversation was short or long, there was always one memory among many mentioned that touched each griever the most—one memory that seemed to exemplify to him the total grief, one memory he related in touching detail where other memories were vague.

Psychologists call it "selective inattention," which means the unconscious selection of one memory against the unconscious inattention to another. We remember best what we want to remember: sometimes to feed an unhealthy guilt; sometimes to soften an unbearable sense of loss; sometimes to cleanse a festering wound; and sometimes to weave happy memories into a creative force for the future.

In accepting the loss of a loved one, every griever brings what he was to his grief and recovers in rhythm to his own character. And no recovery is complete if you think of recovery as a total erasure of grief, for it cannot be. The reason is simple. No one individual can be replaced. When I speak of recovery, I speak of reaffirming your own life and your own future.

And since there is great value in the sharing of experiences, if only to seek a parallel to your own, let us consider what all grievers have in common and then share the recollections and opinions of a few.

A quiet conversation with any griever turns inevitably to his grief, and the despair, held under control so often, so well, will not remain hidden. Again and again, I saw that time and distance are not the palliatives we assure ourselves they are. It is what we do with the time and distance that counts. But before we can do anything it helps to look backward in order to be able even to begin to move forward. That is what grief is all about. The slow progress through shock, suffering, and recovery. The reassessment of self. Little use to say: "I refuse to think about the past." You will anyway, so why not use the memory as nature intended—to give direction to your future.

We all have black moments of icy despair; the wild desire to resurrect the dead, if only for an instant to say, "Did you know how much I loved you?" or "Please forgive me for every hurt I inflicted on you—for every unkind word—for every impatience."

We all wonder why it happened to us, and in facing life without a loved one we all say, "What's life all about?" We all move through the numbed weariness of shock and we all suffer in one way or another and we all make mistakes in judgment—the wrong decisions. We all yearn to forget, not knowing how. And we all find courage we did not know we had and it surprises us and our friends.

We all move in dreamlike step, tentatively, as if we are walking on hot coals, and we would give anything to share the grief; escape the loneliness; run for cover. But we rarely do anything more drastic than suffer be-cause we are afraid to die, although there comes a flash of time when we would like to die and we say: "What is the use of going on?" But most of us do go on, weep-ing for the dead and for ourselves, and ashamed of our self-pity as if it were a sin. And we all grasp a comfort-ing thought: "I'm glad his suffering is over" or "He would have hated to be an invalid" or "Everything happens for the best" or "It is God's will" or "What is to be will be."

And yet, hard as we try, as cheerful as we appear, the ache of grief returns again and again. Recently I received a telephone call from a widow. She told me of her summer plans. They were busy and complicated plans and she spoke with enthusiasm until we were about to say goodbye and then she said: "I know it sounds great, but mentally I feel awful."

That is the way grief moves. It spirals up, it spirals down, and then it lurks at the periphery of our lives, leaving us different from those who have never been touched by its coming. Stronger, more understanding, softer, mellowed by suffering. When I say "all of us," I mean the majority. There are the exceptions, of course.

Suicide is one such exception. When we think of suicide, we think of someone momentarily insane, someone who is willing to destroy himself for revenge against society. We assume he is saying, "I'll show them —they'll be sorry!" But doctors and psychologists know that no answer is as simple as that. There are other motives for suicide: hopelessness, a sense of failure, helplessness, a sense of isolation, the worry of being a burden to others, and even a determination to end suffering—all these can be motives for suicide. Here is a suicide note written by a young divorcée whose little girl died.

She wrote: "This is the tenth night, I've sat in this

empty room holding this little bottle of sleeping pills. Why don't I swallow them, why do I wait? Why do I write all this down? Because I want to talk—I need to talk. I wish I felt bitter like I did when Jim and I were divorced. Then it was just anger and disappointment. Yes, that's how it was then. Whatever the pain of it I didn't expect it to last. That's the important part. I could cry then, I can't cry now. When Penny died everyone said: 'You are taking it so well. You're wonderful! So brave!' Isn't that a laugh? Complimenting me for being a Zombie!

"Suicide has an ugly sound. They'll say I was immature, insane, hostile. But I say it will be the end of unbearable pain. Just that and no more. I don't feel immature, insane or hostile. I just ache. It isn't a dull ache, it's a roaring active pain, tossing and turning at my insides; digging and clawing at my body until I feel trapped into a tight corner—and there's no escape.

"If grief is just an emotion, why does it hurt so much physically? And why doesn't it stop? 'Time will heal' —everyone said that. Heal the pain? Is that what they mean? Then it isn't an emotion after all since 'it' will heal like a bruise. I wonder. To me grief is not an emotion nor a bruise. Grief is a monster who wraps you in straps of steel, twisting them ever tighter about your body until you scream in anguish, but it is all invisible. You are invisible. And so alone. And time crawls by and your pain increases. It goes on and on, deeper and deeper until finally you sit alone, desperate to end the agony, and before you know it, you've found the sleeping pills and for a moment you're almost free—just thinking of that quiet sleep that will kill the pain once and for all. And yet you hesitate. I'm afraid to die. Why am I so afraid? But I'm more afraid to live——"

That was the end of the note. She chose to die.

You see? This woman's thoughts were reasonable, her emotions raw; her hope for a future undefined and bleak. How sad that such a state is temporary and she did not know it.

You may call her weak, even deranged, but I believe she was caught and trapped in what many grievers feel, if only momentarily, but never admit. Therefore it is an extension of normal grief—luckily the exception.

The "solitary mourner" either by choice or because the family is small and scattered has the saddest climb to recovery. One day I was shopping in a New York department store. The saleslady was a charming woman. And somehow our conversation turned from dresses to her grief. She said:

"My husband died suddenly. Heart attack. I didn't know what to do. Wouldn't see anyone. I didn't even get a call from some of our friends. Everyone was pretty nice at the funeral, then—nothing. So I stayed home for months. I'd walk around the apartment and touch the lovely things he'd bought for me on our travels. He was a fine musician, played with the best orchestras. Everyone loved him.

"Do you know theatrical people? Well they're

nice and friendly but they're busy and where did I fit in after George died? Nowhere. Finally the doctor gave me a good talking to. He said: 'You want to kill yourself? Now get out and get a job. Find something. Sell. Try it, what've you got to lose?' So I tried it, and I like it. I'm not alone any more. I'm dead tired at night, so I sleep. Everybody has a problem. I see that now. I've made new friends—even see some of the old friends. Part of it was my fault. I expected too much, didn't I?"

If you look at her story, it seems inconsistent. She refused to see anyone and was hurt because she did not. So many stories are like that. Friends want to see you before you are ready and when you are ready they have disappeared. When will we learn that sometimes a griever needs to withdraw and then needs attention? Is the pattern too hard to understand or is it too inconvenient for us?

Generally speaking, widowers remarry quicker than widows. Is it because their love is not as deep or because there are so many widows and divorcées of all ages available? Not necessarily. One widower explained it this way:

"My life is a shambles. I know little about cooking, less about cleaning. I leave an empty house in the morning and come back to an empty house at night. We were married one week after we graduated from college. I'm used to coming home to life. I'd open the front door and call: 'Hi! Honey, I'm home!' and usually she'd come from the kitchen. 'Hi, Sweetie!' she'd say. A woman's voice, her smile, her—well, her femininity. I'd change my clothes—get into slacks, an old comfortable jacket—read the paper—relax. We'd have a cocktail. She'd move in and out of the kitchen and though I didn't watch her, I knew she was there. Then we'd eat together and I'd tell her what happened at the office.

"God, how I miss her—her perfume, yes, and that great clutter of stuff a woman collects, you know, creams and make-up . . . The way she worried about me, a man misses that. She'd say: 'Are you *sure* you're not too tired to go to the movies?' or 'Why don't you take a nap before we go out tonight?'

"After fifteen years of traveling everywhere together, by car, train or plane, can you imagine the way I felt traveling alone for the first time? Oh, I'd taken business trips alone—but that's different. I knew she was at home. I knew she was waiting for me. I'd call. 'How did it go?' she'd ask. 'When will you be home?'

"The worst of it is, now I don't care about anything or anyone. I hired a woman to clean and when I come home our place looks almost as it used to look. But it doesn't . . . It is cold and empty."

He will marry soon, not because he loved less but because he loved deeply. He will be criticized by some who do not realize his needs, but that is their problem, not his.

Grievers who worry too much about what people will say or do say are wasting precious time. A young widow said: "Everyone told me I must not cry in front of my six-year-old daughter. It would leave such emotional scars. I took that advice. It was bad advice. One day she asked me: 'You're glad Daddy died, aren't you Mommy? Why didn't you love Daddy?' Believe me after we'd cried together, things were a lot easier for both of us. You can't fool children—why try?"

You can't fool children—but how often can we fool ourselves? Here is an example of a widow who had denied any negative emotions during the suffering stage of grief. She had recovered enough to find a job and return to a social life but she was deeply depressed. She had adored her husband but one night, now a widow for eighteen months, she found herself staring angrily at his picture. She began to shout: "Why did you do this to me? How could you leave me alone like this?" In a blind fury, she snatched the picture off the dresser and hurled it to the floor. "Damn you— damn—damn you!"

The next day she was talking to a psychiatrist. "Why do you condemn yourself for feelings?" he asked. "Intellectually, you know your husband didn't die to punish you. But when he died you did feel abandoned. That is a normal reaction. Finally you've faced your real feelings. Let's talk about what else you feel."

She discovered that she had repressed all her negative emotions: anger, hostility, guilt, self-pity, because they made her feel "wrong." After she understood they were normal reactions, she sighed and said: "I've lost eighteen months hiding from myself!"

Does it sound too simple? One visit with a psychiatrist and she stopped hiding from herself? I thought so. I talked about it with another psychiatrist and he pointed out that she had broken through her own self-deception before she even went to the psychiatrist.

The floodgates of negative emotions were already open. All she needed was reassurance. "Most grievers don't need psychoanalysis," he said. "They are depressed by a very real traumatic experience, rather than vague anxieties. Only when a person cannot resolve his grief; face all the negative and positive emotions; and learn to function as a whole person again —then he may need analysis."

"I know a man who needs help," I said.

"You can't decide for anyone else," the psychiatrist smiled. "It must be *his* motivation."

"I know."

I left his office thinking of Tom, hoping he would seek help soon.

Two years ago Tom and his wife Anne were driving through Virginia on their way to Florida for a vacation. He had just been made vice-president of his bank, so their mood was a very happy one. "I'd worked in that bank all my life," he said. "Started at the bottom. Anne was excited—you'd think we'd won a sweepstake. We talked and laughed and I stepped on the gas because the road was empty. 'Let's try water skiing,' I said. 'Be fun, what say, are you game?'

" 'Why not?' Anne giggled. 'Can't you just picture me . . .' She began to wave her arms from side to side, sort of swaying back and forth. I think she was trying to show me how funny she'd look skiing.

"Then I heard a strange banging and her yell. I slammed down hard on the brake but I was going pretty fast. When I ran back she was in a ditch. She was—dead. I knew it, but I acted as if she were alive. I picked her up and cradled her in my arms, rocking back and forth. Finally a car stopped and I said, 'We need a doctor!'

"Funny thing, we always were conservative. The whole bit, locked doors, safety belts. Just that day we were too happy . . .

"After her death, every decision I made was wrong. My judgment was gone. I couldn't stand living in our house. I blamed myself for her death but I couldn't talk to anyone about it. All during her funeral service, I half expected to be picked up by the police for murder. I became withdrawn. I cannot recall one word anyone said to me. I went back to work a few days later—just to get out of the house. I know I was rude and unfriendly—even cynical. I began to feel guilty about my job too, because Anne had waited so many years for me to become vice-president. Again I couldn't talk about it. I was on a treadmill. I worked, went home and stayed alone. I had a nervous breakdown. I was in the hospital for a long time. I came out rested, yes, but restless. I sold my house, resigned from the bank. That's why I'm here in New York."

He didn't find solace in New York and the last I heard of him, he was moving to California. His experience was a ghastly one, and yet, was not his wife as guilty as he? If he had forgotten safety belts and flipping safety buttons, so had she. But then, an all-pervading and persistent guilt is not logical.

Is grief logical? We are mortal and we do die, and when we die someone mourns. That is logical. The patterns of grief are logical, the shock, the suffering, the slow recovery. Life and Death have logic. But we refuse to accept the patterns of grief or the logic of Life and Death. We twist away from the truth; refuse to feel what we feel; deny the need to grieve; and demand a quick recovery. We even have a time-limit for grief—one year. A man-made, arbitrary timing that is senseless and devoid of any understanding of an individual's needs. Should we pretend grief if we have recovered in six months? Should we pretend recovery if we are still suffering after two years?

Once in a great while, I have talked with a level-headed, nonconforming griever who speaks openly and without pretense.

One of these candid grievers is a widow who had also been a divorcée. Asked to describe the difference in her feelings between the two, she thought for a long moment, and then she said: "After my divorce from Philip I was full of self-doubt. I wasted time reliving every second of our marriage wondering where I had failed. If others could succeed in marriage, why couldn't I? And yet I hoped for a reconciliation. It was a vague hope, but a hope just the same. We never did reconcile.

"Then I married Ken. God, how happy we were! When he died, well, no hope for reconciliation this time. Death is so final, isn't it? But at least I know it wasn't my fault—that is the big difference.

"My first marriage failed slowly, but here in the midst of a busy, happy life, Ken was gone—snuffed out like a candle. Poof!

"Our house is a rattling old barn, where it used to feel like a cosy cottage. Traveling alone is miserable, where it was a joy together. Even food has become a necessary evil rather than a time for a companionable exchange of ideas. It's a frightfully dull life, a widow's life, but that terrible sense of failure I had after my divorce—that I don't have at all.

"You may not understand this, but when Ken died his body was cremated. I keep his ashes in our bedroom. It comforts me to know part of him is still with me. It shocks many of my friends, but what of it? Are they with me through the dreary nights? It's a rhetorical question. They are not."

How openly she admitted her sense of failure after

the divorce, her sense of helplessness after Ken's death. How admirable her strength in keeping Ken's ashes where she needed them. And in shocking her friends, has she lost them? Not at all. She is a woman who expects people to accept her as she is. And they do.

Most grievers feel that losing a husband, a wife, or a child is the worst grief because you lose a great slice of your own life at the same time. But suppose you are an unmarried daughter, living at home, and one of your parents die. Is not that, too, a great slice of your life?

I talked with one young girl who asked to see me. She was twenty years old and told her story in a clipped manner rather than the way most people grope for words to express their feelings. "I've never spoken of this to anyone," she said. "I think I'll feel better when I do—that's why I asked to see you. It happened suddenly just a year ago. It was after midnight. Daddy was breathing heavily, his arms and legs were ice cold, and his face looked like a mask—all gray. I was frightened.

"I called the doctor. Mother was very quiet and brave, but how long could she hold up?

"I heard wheels on the gravel. I dashed downstairs and let the doctor in.

"One glance at my dad and the doctor hurried to the phone; ordered an ambulance; had the hospital alerted.

"Then I heard wailing sirens. How would they cope

with an unconscious man on the third floor of a house with narrow twisting stairs? They decided that the only way to get Daddy into the ambulance was to use a sheet as a lowering cradle down the stairwell. When I saw my father handed down like a laundry basket, I knew how ill he was and how unlikely his recovery would be.

"How could I live without his moral and emotional support? I told myself he'd live, but he died.

"I found that a mental breakdown or maturity is the end result of such a situation. There were weeks when no gambler would have taken odds either way.

"The discipline of a job and seeing that despite Mother's grief she had proper meals, brought me around to at least a dull acceptance of the situation."

She had talked quickly. Now she sighed. "I feel better," she said. "Thank you for listening."

All grievers need to talk. Feelings expressed become less frightening and easier to accept. Death does not always destroy only good relationships; sometimes the griever has lost a relationship which was abnormally ambivalent, divisive and unsatisfactory. All the more reason the griever needs to talk because his grief holds many conflicting emotions.

A grieving father said: "My son died three months ago. He was thirty-five years old, that's all. I can't get over it. But I shouldn't feel this way. We didn't get along. He drank, you see. He drank himself to death. He didn't have to die, but he couldn't stop drinking.

"He was an engineer—a good one. Earned good pay.

So smart, except when he saw a bottle. He was a nice guy, basically good. I always hoped he'd snap out of it —that drinking. His wife left him. He lived with me for a while, but I had to tell him to move—who can live with a guy who's bashed every weekend? He wouldn't join AA. He wouldn't stop drinking. I don't understand. I never touch the stuff. Why did he need it?"

This father's anger, love, and guilt needed more than a friend's interest. He needed professional help and decided to get it.

There are all too many stories of parents whose children died under tragic circumstances. Accidental deaths, some avoidable, others unavoidable, but no other grief is as haunted by guilt as a child's death. Parents blame themselves whether they are blameless or not. It is the most poignant grief and inconsolable. Even professionals like ministers and psychologists grope to find a rationale for a child's death that can reach grieving parents. Here the stages of grief are prolonged, the pain of loss beyond comprehension.

If the parents can talk about their child's death with each other, and together seek professional help, that is considered a vital key to recovery.

I believe this cross-section of stories shows how memory can haunt the living and how each anecdote holds its own poignancy. Whether you grieve for a close friend, a child, a brother or sister, a husband or wife or parent, you emerge chastened by the experience—and the closer the relationship the wider the gap left in your life by the death of a loved one.

On the anniversary of his father's death, a son wrote a letter to his mother. He was in military service stationed across the country. He had flown home just before his father died. He wrote:

"Dear Mom,

"I wish I could be with you, especially now. I hope my letters give you some idea of how aware I am of the 'peaks and troughs' of your days. Well, you are such a wise woman, you don't need a pep talk from me, but I am with you and rooting for you all the time.

"It's funny that recurring thoughts of Dad have increased since our son Tommy was born—especially my sadness that they cannot know each other. My son will have no memory or identity for such a relationship. Perhaps he'll know Dad because he'll know me. Everyone says I'm much like him, do you think so too?

"There is a moment of time when the loss of someone as close as Dad was to me has little relationship with grief. As you know, I spent my share of hours sitting in the room with him before he died. When it was over, there was no special feeling—it is as though I had adjusted and made my peace during those last hours.

"One thought troubled me. When Dad had told me about the operation, I told him, I hoped he would check carefully before he had it. How I wish I had stopped it from happening, which is a feeling of guilt, isn't it?

During the agony of receiving relatives and friends, I was, or felt, singularly alone. This is to say in terms of someone I could really communicate with. Later I was upset by all the rituals—meeting with the minister; the endless hours of sitting, waiting for events; the preoccupation with funeral arrangements, the cars, the stream of unimportant people to obstruct the normal process of saying goodbye emotionally to someone we loved. I didn't know how to help you; wouldn't know how again if history could repeat itself; and I'm not sure anyone can know the best approach. I was there—maybe that's the only answer.

"The process of adapting to grief was easier for me than for you. I flew back across the country alone—back to my wife, my career and a different environment. You were simply left alone.

"The years you and Dad had were 'quality' stuff, memorable years to cherish. And in your case you have the opportunity now to impart to others that which only you can give.

"Please visit us soon. I could use 'X' days to talk with you as we share a roaring fire.

Love you,
Paul"

This young man said his farewells to his father in the hospital room. And while he was "upset" by the rituals that followed, these rituals were a necessary procedure for those who hadn't been in that hospital room.

There seems to be a human need to define the finality of death in order to help the griever accept the death as a truth. Isn't that why parents and wives of men killed in battle want the bodies sent home? Proof, final proof.

After you have accepted the death and your own emotions, whatever they are, and you begin to reorganize your own life, you will find that the love you gave to the one who is gone needs to be given to many. Rather than a search for one substitute, offer your interest and concern wherever and whenever you see a need. All these people you met in this chapter were left with an untapped reservoir of love.

I recommended earlier that for awhile you dwell on your memories, even allow yourself self-pity or any other emotional reaction you feel—but once done, there come the days of redirection and belief in your own life—in life itself.

Your grief becomes part of your secret inner life, and out of its suffering can emerge a new and vital you —because you worked through the stages of grief to make it so.

Chapter Six

GRIEF, LONELINESS,
AND SEX

W<small>HEN</small> you begin to tick off the areas in which grievers have nowhere to turn for advice, it is unbelievable, shocking. And sex is another obstacle they must hurdle alone.

What can I possibly say about sex that has not already been said? Nothing, if you think in terms of the very young. But if you think in terms of the widow and widower, very little has been said. The subject has been wrapped in silence, and as with so many aspects of grief, the widow and widower are left to muddle along in the best way they can.

I wondered if the widows and widowers, once past their early grief, would be reluctant to discuss sexual needs, desires, hopes, or experiences. I felt it might be construed as an invasion of privacy so I avoided any

direct question about sex, only to discover I was col-
lecting a vast amount of material from both men and
women in ages ranging from thirty to seventy-five.
Oh, you thought grandma or grandpa was too old?
Resigned, maybe. Tossed into celibacy, often. But in-
competent? Only when it is a lifelong disinterest, or
illness erases the sexual needs as it does other appetites.

The more people we interviewed, the more we realized that sex was an important factor in every widow
and widower's life, no matter what their ages, and that
for some unknown reason was rarely, if ever, mentioned in articles, books, or even in our interviews with
doctors, psychiatrists, and ministers.

I spoke to a typist who was doing some work for me,
a woman I had never met. "If you ask me," she said,
"there's no need to write about sex and the widow.
Widowers, yes, they need it for their egos. But when a
widow is past thirty, she needs hard work, nothing
else!" Yet given an iota of encouragement, the widows
and widowers wanted to talk about their sexual problems. One young man offered this bit of information: "I
have little sex drive, don't know why, but there it is. I
doubt if I'll ever remarry."

In contrast, a young widow said, "My husband and
I had a good sex life. Since he passed away, I've lived
like a virgin. My minister was evasive when I mentioned my sense of frustration. He gave me that 'Now,
now, my dear,' but I got his message: 'Respectable
women shouldn't have such desires, it isn't nice.' "

Some widows may give up right then and there and

spend the rest of their lives trying to suppress normal desires to prove they are respectable. Of course there are people who can live very comfortably without either sex or marriage. Just as there are a few who choose to banish the very idea of second marriage. One man said: "For me it's one marriage, one mate. That's that!"

A similar opinion is more formally expressed by Jean Z. Owen:

Sex relationship is a basic factor in a sound and happy marriage; yet when the husband dies, the need for sex expression disappears almost completely, unless the widow keeps her libido active by constantly dwelling on the subject or by seeking masculine company exclusively. A true frustration does exist in many cases, but almost invariably it has a mental or emotional basis. . . . Guilt is another underlying factor that masquerades as physical desire. . . . But the third and most common basis for a feeling of physical frustration is an unwillingness to relinquish youth.*

I do not know what kind of widows Miss Owen interviewed to arrive at the foregoing conclusions. I suspect, however, that the widows we interviewed were either more normal or more honest. They told us that after living through the first stage of shock and numbness, their sexual desires returned. The major problem was what to do about them.

Recently a widow was trying to forget that it was

* From *Widows Can Be Happy* (New York: Greenberg, 1950), p. 134. Used with permission.

April, the month in which her husband had died two years before, but she did not succeed. As the anniversary day drew closer, her depression grew deeper, her mood preoccupied. Late one evening during this period, when the phone rang, she jumped as she had jumped when her husband lay dying in the hospital and she had been sent home for a few hours' rest. "I'm sorry. He's gone," the doctor had said that terrible night. Somehow, caught between remembering the past and the now-jangling bell, she ran toward the phone and tripped. She knew before she looked that she had broken her ankle. For the next few weeks, she was forced to stay at home. Finally, it was the second anniversary of her husband's death. She had no engagement, preferring to protect all her friends from seeing the despair she could hide most of the time. Unexpectedly a man called whom she had been seeing and liked, a gentle kindly man, who asked if he could drop by for a little while.

"Do come," she said. She glanced into the mirror, hoping he would believe the pale drawn look of her was because of her broken ankle.

When he arrived, they talked about his teaching and her teaching, politics, and then about her injury. All at once they were silent and he put an arm across her shoulders and tipped her head and kissed her. There was something about him that stirred a long-sleeping emotion. She glanced at his face expecting to find what she had found in a few other unwanted faces. That I-want-you look that had nothing to do with love as she had known it. But his look was good.

As the kissing led to caresses and the caresses led to deeper emotions, he lifted her into his arms and carried her into the bedroom. There was a comforting manliness in his action, a long lost tenderness in his voice, and then his hand touched her face—"Darling, what's the matter?" There was real concern in his tone. She opened her eyes and ran her own hand along her cheek. She was crying soundlessly, she had not even known the tears were there. "Please, darling, what is it?" he asked again.

"My husband died two years ago—tonight."

"I wouldn't hurt you, you know that." He stroked her hair as if she were a little girl. "But I can't let you hurt me, either."

"I haven't heard from him since," she told me. "He was a dear man, but obviously I am still in love with my husband. That night I was in an absolute panic—anything to forget." She sighed. "People say when you are a widow you should never say 'never,' but I'm convinced that for me sex and marriage must go together."

Except for a few grievers who because of illness or temperament preferred to live alone, most of those we interviewed were dissatisfied with the prospects of living alone, unloved and unloving, for the rest of their lives.

After all, our society is geared to the married, and a widow or widower is plunged into an existence long-since forgotten, the highly competitive life of the single: a life the griever neither understands nor desires because it belongs to the past, as do college, blind dates, and the intricacies of youthful courtship. The adventurous search for a mate is an integral part of youth, but as a griever, the search lacks camaraderie and spirit. No longer an adventure, it sinks into a forlorn journey through an alien and lonely world.

When a mate dies, the marriage feels to the survivor as real as if it still existed for quite a while. And yet the sexual appetites of healthy males and females are only dulled by grief. Once over the initial shock and suffering, they discover the sex drive goes on and the choice of how it goes on is theirs. Unfortunately, the widow finds she is a social burden, one of all too many unattached females. At first she is only interested in male *companionship*, someone with whom to share an evening, but she soon learns that her friends and relatives accept her as a loner, or they just do not know any available males. She becomes the one who fills out a dinner table when someone's wife is ill or away, or she is invited to join a couple for dinner and a movie. Sometimes she is approached by a married man whose attitude is "what my wife doesn't know won't hurt her," since he assumes that, once widowed, she is pitifully eager to share her bed. And sometimes, even worse for her ego, she is not approached by anyone at all.

A distressing problem that confronts the widow is the change of attitude toward her of other widows once they have married again. They move back into the married world and forget their widowed friends. But then in most cases, so does everyone else. They do not forget her as a person, just as an eligible one.

If your social group would unite to make a project of finding eligible males for you to date, they would evince far more compassion than in accepting you as a widow and idly hoping that you would remarry—someday. These same friends would be shocked to hear you were frequenting bars to meet men. And they would be right. It is not an effective procedure for a mature woman.

As a rule the help she needs she does not get. Of course there are exceptions. I know several widows who have been introduced to eligible men by their friends. It just does not happen often enough.

One day, I was sitting on the beach between two married women who had just met. "I wish I knew someone for you," one of them said to me, "but I don't." I nodded. It was such a familiar remark. Then she and the other woman began to exchange the names of people they both knew in the city. Within a few minutes, they had mentioned among mutual friends at least three widowers. There you have it. It was amusing because even after mentioning these men, they seemed to forget I was still sitting there. I could only guess that they both had sisters or cousins or closer friends whom they considered more suitable for the widowers, or they just did not want to get involved.

The problems of widowhood are very difficult to imagine and that is part of the horror, the unexpected devastation. The loss of status. This is a world of men *and* women until the woman is a widow, and then it is a world of women. To me, it is no longer surprising that desperation causes some widows to be known as aggressive, predatory females.

At a dinner party, a widow leaned across the table addressing the man opposite her. "Which of these lovely ladies is your wife?" she asked.

"Unfortunately, none," he said. "I'm a widower."

"Are you listed in the phone book?" she asked immediately. Just like that. No subtlety.

Another widower was invited to a cocktail party. He had known the widowed hostess for years, but casually. As the guests began to leave she asked him to stay. He assumed to help clean up and he agreed. Once alone, she said: "George, I think we should get married."

He was shocked to put it mildly, but he said, "Why do you think so?"

"We have so much in common," she said.

They did not get married and he felt rather shaken but untouched by the experience. In truth they did not have "so much in common" and he, like most men, retreated from such flagrant pursuit.

Both of these women were aware of the dearth of available men and desperate. Thus are aggressive, predatory females born.

The widower's problems are vastly different. He

is swamped with invitations. He often resists. After years of marriage he may feel reluctant to return to the insecurity of calling for a date or pursuing a woman as if he were a youngster. His solution is in marrying someone he has known for years or a widow, friend of a friend, so he can move back into the routine of marriage as quickly as possible. When he does marry a young girl, the psychologists feel he is trying (unconsciously) to escape his own aging and hopes to regain the joys of youth, even a new family of children. But generally speaking, the average widower prefers a quiet courtship, devoid of stress and strain, with a woman from his own social and economic background.

This does not suggest that a widower's life is an easy one. It just suggests that if he reaches the stage of wanting female companionship, a love affair or remarriage, the supply of available females is abundant. Socially, the odd man is an asset. Socially, the odd woman is a liability.

Aristotle said: "To live alone, one must either be an animal or a god." Harsh words and not always true, but perhaps this is why, as the shock and suffering of grief lessens, some grievers feel the need for the opposite sex in many different ways. Most of all they miss the importance of their roles as husband and wife, for when the partnership of marriage is suddenly destroyed by death, the griever has lost his role in life and his "love object" at one and the same time. It is an intolerable deprivation even when the marriage was less than ideal.

And right here is where the equality of the sexes bogs down completely. The widow's problem in finding a new mate is statistical. Beyond the age of twenty-five, women outnumber men in all age groups, and widows outnumber widowers in some areas of America eight to one.

These people need answers. They need guidance. They need help. A sudden interruption in a normal sex life presents deep and complicated problems. Sandwiched between the trauma of a mate's death and remarriage or resignation into living alone, there is a gap of long empty months, even years, a gap which should be lifted out of the silence to which it has been relegated so that widows and widowers have the opportunity to know what happens to people as loners; how they solve or fail to solve sexual problems. Open discussions on sexual behavior could prepare grievers on how to decide what they, as individuals, would do or would not do when they are confronted with dates. It is the lack of knowledge that leads them into rejecting or accepting new alliances at the wrong time and in the wrong way.

Second marriages can be happy, creative, and fulfilling, but we are dealing with the sexual lull between death and remarriage, or death and the acceptance of life alone. It is during this lull that errors in judgment are made, out of ignorance.

There are no easy answers. Just as psychiatrists agree there is not a completely normal individual, they also agree there is not a standard sex drive. Because our sexual capacities are as individual as our finger-prints, any value judgment on how people feel about sex and what they want sexually would be a fool-hardy step. No doubt if we could have interviewed thousands instead of hundreds, the stories would still vary from those who reject sex as unimportant to those who suffer immeasurably without it.

You cannot always solve your sexual or remarriage problems, but there is value in knowing what you want and why. It clears the clutter of thinking if you know the truth about yourself, especially if you accept what you are and what you feel without shame or dismay. You may decide to sublimate desires, or compromise in selecting a new mate. You may decide not to subli-mate or compromise. But whatever you decide, if it emerges out of truth, it has a far better chance of suc-cess.

Despite a current separation of sex from love and marriage, guilt still plagues the widow and widower after a brief sexual affair. Psychologists' offices bulge with patients who seek sexual partners only to find they are caught by feelings of anxiety and guilt later.

"It is the inevitable tug of war between animalistic and emotional desires," a psychologist said. "Every man and woman yearns above all else to be loved with-out any reservation for what he really is. Until such a love is found, each man and woman must ask himself: 'What is *my* moral code?' "

A great percentage of widows and widowers were far more interested in companionship or marriage than in brief affairs. They spoke of sex as a natural and healthy part of love—in marriage. The widows who "slept around," as they put it, did so for a variety of reasons. "It's the only way to get dates," or "What am I supposed to do with the rest of my life?"

One man who had been a widower for four years said, "Whenever I'm invited to a friend's house, I know there will be a dinner partner for me—a divorcée or a widow. I feel particularly sorry for widows. They are a drug on the market. Sure I'm searching for a wife, looking all the time. If I meet a gal I'm attracted to, I invite her to lunch. Don't waste much time that way. If she says 'Yes,' fine; if she says 'No,' I don't care."

There are love affairs that seem to work out very well. In one case a widow and widower were casual friends and eased into sexuality before their marriage. Since furtiveness was not necessary, it was a relaxed relationship. "We had lived together for three years," the woman said.

"Frankly I don't think people our age [fifties] should marry without living together first," the man added. "I could have been impotent. She could have been frigid. We could have been incompatible in other ways too."

A griever's readiness for remarriage or sexual involvement is not predictable. Many widows and widowers who have been happily married just have not recovered enough after two, three, even four years to be interested in anyone else.

Oscar is an example of this. His wife died in a plane crash. "My main emotion was bitterness," he said. "I resented every woman I met, I guess because she was alive. Well, regardless of my feelings of grief and anger, I needed a woman sexually. Okay, I'd pay for one. No involvement. A guy in my office gave me the phone number of an expensive call girl. $100. We met at a bar. I was pleasantly surprised. She was young, beautiful, immaculate. A stunner. We had a few drinks and dinner, and when she said, 'Ready to go to my place now?' I think I did a double take. I'd forgotten she was a pro. She lived in a good neighborhood and her apartment was well furnished—only a little pretentious. She flipped on the hi-fi and soft seductive music seemed to float around me. I was a little drunk—but not much.

"As we started to make love, I felt great waves of desire and then, suddenly, great waves of guilt. I tried to force that guilty feeling away but no use. I was impotent for the first and last time in my life. I paid her and went home. I didn't go out again until a friend found the "perfect" woman for me. I liked her. She was mature, good-natured, nice. I married her."

Then there is Virginia, who is still in love with her husband although he has been dead for two years. Fighting depression, she went to California for a change of scene. Her letter reads:

"I know I'm not ready for marriage. All comparisons to Bill are so odious that it could never be a healthy relationship. When I can honestly put him and our life together to rest, perhaps I'll be ready to accept a compromise. In a childish way I want to be taken out and complimented, but I don't want to be touched. Either I haven't met the right kind of man for me, or I will never be able to love again."

There is another side to the sexual coin: the married couples who drift into a listless sex life. One widower, Jim, said frankly: "Nancy and I had fallen into a rut. It started when the children were little and my wife was involved with them and I was deeply involved in making good. You know the routine: heavy mortgage, two cars, good schools for the kids. Our sex life became matter of fact. You could mark it off on a calendar—once a week, once a month and then once in a great while. We loved each other but the romance of it was—well, over. When Nancy died the children were away at college. I was alone and lonely. About six months later I was introduced to Alison. We went out about a dozen times. Remember, I'm almost fifty now. But one night after a movie, we walked along Fifth Avenue, hand in hand, and all at once I wanted her—so much. At her apartment I didn't leave as I had done before. I didn't hurry her, and at first she seemed nervous. Slowly her passion matched mine and I was shocked by my own virility. Nothing matter of fact in this union. We're like two kids . . . ."

I asked Jim if he thought Alison would talk with me. "I'll ask," he said. "No names used—right?"

When I saw Alison I was very surprised. This was

no glamour gal. She was frankly and openly middle-aged. A charming person, petite and slim. "It's a miracle," she said. "I'd only had a few dates since my husband died. And each time, after just one evening, the man expected to stay all night. I'm too old-fashioned for that sort of thing. Besides, they didn't seem to like me very much. I felt like a new restaurant they were willing to try. From the beginning, Jim was different. Friendly and interested. We enjoy quiet times—museums, concerts. I feel he respects me as much as I respect him. I think we're in love. Isn't that wonderful?"

Are they going to marry? I do not know, but my guess would be yes, easily and without planning. For the moment they have found each other and that seems to be enough.

Not all widows and widowers fall into such a happy situation. Some we interviewed told of harrowing experiences. If you are a widow or widower who had been married for years, it sometimes comes as a shock to find a lover whose sexual needs are so different from what you have known. The very act becomes a crushing blow.

Although sometimes a love affair can save a damaged ego, especially if you have been lonely for a long time.

Most widowers summed up their sex lives with one sentence: "I play the field." But the follow-up interviews show they do not play the field very long. The widower usually remarries, if he is going to remarry at all, within months, or a year or two, after his wife's death.

The widow takes far longer to remarry, sometimes out of choice, sometimes because she has no choice at all. An odd story came from Inez, a widow with three small children. She was consoled by a bachelor in his forties. "He was very attentive," she said, but as her grief abated, she was aware that in all the months they had dated constantly, he had only kissed her on the forehead. What was at first a blessing became an annoyance later. She began to ask discreet questions here and there, but no one knew much about him personally, except that he still lived with his mother. "Sexually, I'd call him a neuter," she said. She shrugged. "It's all right. It gave me time to recover and now it gives me an entrée into dinner parties and dances that I couldn't get to alone. He's the kind of man most widows would enjoy, especially in the first few years, because he's so gentle and gallant."

Obviously they were not a happy twosome because their sexual needs were incompatible. However, a real platonic friendship between a mature man and woman is not only possible but a good solution for those who enjoy the opposite sex, but have sexual standards which make love affairs without marriage wrong for them. Together they can enter that wonderful world of man plus woman when they go for a walk or a movie or she entertains him at home. In conversation they can share the male and female viewpoints, even confidences. This kind of companionship can be an oasis for both of them, stimulating and interesting; but only if they both want to share time with each other without sharing the responsibility and emotional involvement of a love affair or marriage.

The search for a new love as you hold fast to the old is a distressing experience. Carl was a widower. He said: "I'd been seeing this woman, and one night she made it quite clear that she wasn't against a more intimate relationship. I sat there watching her and my thoughts were so strange. I was remembering my wife. Had we made love one thousand times? I began to add it up like a score. Twenty years—maybe three times a week—closer to three thousand times wasn't it? I remembered the slow sensual quality of it. I remembered one Sunday morning when the kids were away. We sat in the living room doing the Sunday paper's crossword puzzle. Mary leaned over the puzzle, pen poised, asking me questions. 'Who wrote Siddhartha?'

" 'Try Hesse,' I said. I sat with my head back, stroking her arm. She had such smooth skin.

" 'That's it!' She raised her head as if sensing my mood. I loved the way her lips parted and her eyes closed, waiting, knowing I was the aggressor.

"Then I found myself staring at this woman I hardly knew, thinking, 'It's not my way, but what the heck.' "

Let's listen to a widow's thoughts under similar circumstances. She said: "He took me home after a show and asked if he could come in just for a few minutes.

" 'Would you like a drink?'

" 'Yes, I'd like a drink and a kiss.'

"I resented the casual way he said it. He kissed me and I tried to respond but something was wrong. You see he hadn't said he liked me, found me attractive, nothing. He just kissed me. I found his silence a rebuff. I remembered my husband caressing my hair and whispering how lovely I was as he held me close. If only this man had said something, called me darling, even that might have helped."

A psychologist said: "Whenever you change sexual partners, you are bound to compare what was with what is. A new love is at a different time of your life, under different circumstances, with a different human being. Once you enter into a new partnership you have the rare opportunity of avoiding past mistakes and bringing to it the best of what you are now. If that widower wanted to maintain his role as the aggressor, he could have explained his feelings, gently and tactfully. And that widow could have assured the man she liked him but she wasn't sure he liked her, again gently and tactfully. Almost anything those two said in an attempt to help a current situation would have been better than trying to escape into memories. There is a tendency to idealize the dead and in retrospect hold to this idealized image, when, in fact, no sexual partnership is constantly ideal. And those who effect a robust sexual union usually have made many adjustments, one to the other, before they reach a state of sexual compatibility."

Betty's problem was one of sexual deprivation.

"Just what does a woman do with her sexual desires?" she asked me. "After my husband died, a few married men made passes, but I couldn't let myself react. Call it conscience, call it square, but I felt I'd be stealing. Each time, I told myself, 'You have no right to this man,' but I didn't meet anyone, not one widower or divorcé in those endless years.

"I found a job in an art gallery because everyone said a widow must keep busy. If that's supposed to be a panacea, well! Sure I was tired at night. But not every night, not all night, and not during those long week-ends. I was a bundle of nerves. I took tranquilizers. Nothing helped. And then one of those married men came to see me, said he wanted to know if I'd recommend my daughter's college for his daughter. I was friendly but tense, determined. He made notes as I talked. 'Fine,' he said. 'Thanks.' He slid the notebook into his pocket. Simultaneously we stood up and walked together toward my front door. 'You look beautiful,' he said.

" 'Thank you . . .' He took my hand. We faced each other and I prayed for the strength to say: 'Please go now,' but I couldn't move and I couldn't speak.

" 'We're not going to talk about my marriage which you know is a mess or your marriage which was good,' he said. 'We're not going to talk about anything but us. I love you.' Since then he has stayed all night about twice a week and we've had several weekends. Don't ask me how he manages it. I don't know."

These interviews seem to prove, if nothing else, that dating, a love affair, and marriage are far more complex and difficult in the middle years than they ever are in youth. A youngster has the security of his group. All his friends are single when he is single. All his friends are searching for love when he is searching for love. Later, marriage is the norm, and the griever lives at the periphery of his social group until a new pattern is created.

The late Joshua Liebman wrote, in his book *Peace of Mind:* "When death destroys an important relationship, it is essential that someone be found partially capable of replacing that relationship."

Everyone would agree with that premise. Logically and psychologically it makes sense. And most widowers do just that—find someone. But remember the statistics on widows?

Interpreting that "someone" to be a new mate can be a dangerous assumption. I believe that replacing a mate for both widow and widower is virtually impossible during the shock of early grief and for some time later when the griever is lonely, but still incapable of making decisions based on reality rather than illusion. A psychologist said: "Any quick remarriage may be a foolhardy attempt to avoid loneliness."

Are there any exceptions? Of course. There is the griever whose mate was ill for a long, long time, or one whose marriage was very unhappy. In such cases the disorientation is far less, and the survivor is better prepared to reorganize his life within a shorter span of time.

However, the griever who has sustained a tragic loss must beware of a hasty remarriage. Shortly after her husband's death, Laura married a man ten years her junior. "Ray looked so much like my husband," she said. "It seemed perfect, until our honeymoon. I couldn't understand. He was not at all eager to make love. I told myself it was because he'd never been married before. Then after we'd returned from our honeymoon, I left my shop earlier than usual one day and went home. There he was in our bedroom—with another man." It is not unusual for the male homosexual to marry a mature woman, hoping to become heterosexual or for financial security or because he is, in fact, bisexual. More and more, the homosexual is hard to spot. He is often well-educated, muscular, and very masculine acting.

It is easy to understand that the patterns of sexual behavior defy any semblance of predictability. Every griever needs to search for his sexual future based upon his conscience, his self-knowledge, and his goals—a clarity that comes with an open mind, clear self-analysis, and a willingness to keep close watch on his reactions to every situation as it arises.

Joshua Liebman's words "someone . . . capable of replacing" I feel was a generalization. After all, he does not mention sexual activity, a love affair, or a new mate. One cannot compare mature widows and wid-

owers with attitudes of today's youth toward pre-
marital sex, since that would be like comparing the am-
putee with someone who had a tonsillectomy.

The search for sexual fulfillment as a widow or
widower is not all that simple. Therefore, once you
are ready to resume social activities, the best way to
start is with those you already know. It is wise to accept invitations from friends, young and old, single or
married, as often as you can, with or without a date.
Forget you are the fifth wheel. They invited you because they wanted to, and it's far better than sitting
alone staring at those proverbial four walls.

Show them that you are enjoying the evening and
their company and how much you look forward to
seeing them again. Remember the old-fashioned man-
ners that were so endearing? Use them. A phone call
of appreciation is still endearing, and an invitation to
your place gives the necessary continuity to the relationship. I know, you do not feel up to entertaining.
It is not easy, but try to rise above your reluctance.

Encourage your new friendships, never losing contact with old friends. The more you circulate, the
greater your chance to meet new friends. Perhaps a
new mate. But you cannot depend on that. You can
depend on what circulating does for you. It gives you
something to anticipate; the opportunity to practice
techniques of projecting charm and interest; and it reminds friends that you are ready to enjoy life again.

If and when you do have a date and once you have

made it, no matter how low your morale, no matter how depressed you might feel, this is one facet of your life that absolutely demands deception. It is not fair to burden a date with your problems, your disappointments, or your grief.

There are lonely men and lonely women everywhere, yearning to love and be loved; unsure of how and where to find the right one; silent in their bewilderment; shy of admitting their desire for a new life, a new love, a new mate. You are not the only one embarrassed by dating; every mature griever is. And there is one thing for sure, what happens on or after a date depends on the man and woman involved. No one else.

Mature people are more cautious than the very young, usually more sensitive to another's mood. This very maturity gives them both the time to establish a rapport tailored to fit their relationship.

Just prepare for every engagement as if it were an adventure. Do not complain about anything or anyone. It is your responsibility to make the evening as pleasant as possible. Many an evening you will come home sure it was not worth the effort. But it was. Even if you never see that particular man or woman again, the experience is worthwhile. Through it you will grow in independence, in judgment, and in discovering what you want your life to be—socially and sexually.

Chapter Seven

HOW TO HELP
A FRIEND IN GRIEF

Recently when my dad died, one of my friends said, "It must be easier for you, since he lived such a long life."

I was grateful for her unspoken thought that my husband had died years before he had reached old age. But her cheerful words gave me cold comfort. Didn't she realize that when someone you love dies, his death is deeply significant no matter what his age?

How do *you* help a friend in grief? Perhaps you telephone, send flowers to the chapel, or a check to his favorite charity, go to the funeral, invite him to your place once or twice to "buck him up," and then you slip back into your own life, assuring yourself you have done all you could.

That is not enough. A friend in grief needs you desperately, as much and sometimes more than he needs his family, and you, as a friend, have the power to help or hinder his recovery. That is how important you really are. Surprisingly enough, to help effectively takes only a clearer understanding of grief, a little extra time, and a willingness to listen.

As soon as you hear a friend is in grief, phone him. Get to him as quickly as you can. Do not ask him what you can do, ask a member of his family. Once there, be alert. Does he need someone to answer the phone; someone to make calls; send wires; brew coffee; or just sit beside him? Offer physical contact, especially to a woman. Hold her hand, and if when you greet her, she clings, do not be afraid even if you are a happily married man. To her, in shock, you are just a comforting shoulder, no more. Usually in early grief a person acts out of habit much as he did before the death. Therefore, if he wants to talk, no matter what the subject, listen.

If your friend has collapsed and cannot be seen, phone every day, send a few flowers, a thinking-of-you card. Keep in touch.

Bite your tongue before you utter one cliché like "time heals all wounds." That is like telling a starving man he will eat—someday! I hope all such clichés, including the one "each man must work through his own grief," will be discarded along with every other generality. In the final analysis every man does work through his own grief, but he recovers more quickly with supportive and loving friends at his side. A man learns from talking out his problems, not from hoarding them; from being with interested friends, not from staring into empty space. A man turns away from grief only when he feels needed and loved by the living.

One psychiatrist said this: "As a group, Americans are generous and kindly, but as individuals they believe emotion is a sign of weakness and they turn away from anyone emotionally upset, not because they are cruel but because they deny themselves the same emotional responses they deny others."

It seems to be true enough. We applaud a griever who "takes a death very well," and by this we mean he accepts it stoically and goes on living as if nothing much happened. Fine, if it works, but it does not. Someone who lived, no longer lives, someone who was an important figure in the family is beyond reach, and facing this is a traumatic experience. The mystery of death comes too close for comfort. We wonder what happens after death. We wish we had been kinder. We worry—did we do enough to save him? We feel great anxiety, and the more we loved the one who died, the greater the anguish.

A widower expressed his sense of abandonment in this way: "Everyone meant well. They came to see me. The women kissed me on the cheek and whispered, 'I'm so sorry.' The men shook my hand and said, 'If there is anything I can do to help, just let me know.' And then they sat around talking about the weather, even politics. They talked around me and at me, but not *with* me. It was a nightmare."

"What did you want these people to do?" I asked.

"Stop pretending it was a social call. My wife was killed in an automobile accident. I wanted to talk about her."

"Some people cannot bear to talk at a time like that. I am sure your friends thought it would be too painful. How would they know what to say?"

"If they had sat next to me long enough to *listen*—I would have talked about her. That is how they would know!" He sounded angry but there were tears in his eyes, a pleading look in his face.

It is long past time to change our attitude toward the grievers. "Why bother trying to change things," a widow said with a hopeless shrug, "no one will help you!"

"What kind of help do you mean?" I asked.

"Oh, if people would call on the phone regularly to see how I am doing. Listen, I live alone—way out in the country. Once I drove to friends for dinner. When I arrived home, how nice if they had called to make sure I got back all right, that would have been nice, would it not? Little thoughtful things mean so much."

Friends often overlook the terrible passivity that comes with grief. If friends think a griever should "keep busy," how valuable it would be for them to discuss with him what he might be interested in doing. And then how valuable if they would investigate places for him to go, people to see, set up appointments for him, do the "leg work"—get him started. Travel? Yes, but not alone, not in early grief. Travel with friends, or to friends, or with a group.

You see, a griever needs friends who are willing to be involved. In my own grief, my best friend wrote me a letter explaining how upset she was and why she could not see me at all, or even talk to me on the phone. "I know I would break down and make things worse for you," she wrote. "I cannot believe your Kay is dead and I am a wreck thinking about it—please remember I love you." Would it not have been better if she had come and indeed cried with me? The knowledge that a friend loved the one who died and shares your sorrow brings friends closer together. She wouldn't have made it worse for me; on the contrary, she would have made it easier to bear.

Other letters came reminding me of all my happy memories. One said: "When you see a beautiful flower, you will think of your husband and be comforted." How my husband would have chuckled at that idea. All too often, friends give advice that leads you, alone, into unknown places and relieves them of any responsibility. "Join a club," they will say. Now if they would help you join their clubs, or make inquiries about clubs you might enjoy, good and helpful. But a vague suggestion—no.

Many widows are forced to work for the first time. How to help? Offer to find a vocational guidance counselor who can evaluate what she is equipped to do. Or if she has worked before, offer to look into agencies which handle the type of employment she needs. Again, active participation is far better than any vague suggestions.

"I am fortunate," a widower said, after one son was killed in Vietnam. "I have my other children."

"They live nearby?" I asked.

"My daughter lives in England and my other son lives in Arizona. But they keep in touch——" His voice trailed off. I wondered, since he was a widower, what he did with his evenings after work and the long weekends. Letters from England and calls from Arizona could not begin to fill his life.

He had heard the tired cliché, "How fortunate you are to have your children." But was he? In a way. He knew there were two people in the world who really cared about him. That *is* fortunate. Nevertheless, he needed available friends from his own environment to ease his aloneness. It is all right to count your blessings, but be sure you are counting the right ones.

I do not overlook the value of religious faith—a man's belief in God or Destiny or Fate. This is of valid help to many, and alleviates some of the inner turmoil and pain, but it does not come to grips with practical day-to-day living. The question I am asking is this: How can you and I help a friend in grief face the shock, the suffering, and the slow process of recovery?

I was witness to what friends can do to hinder recovery. One bleak day in December I trudged through the windy, snow-packed streets of New York to a neighborhood beauty shop. Tony, the owner, had combed my hair and his wife, Adrianna, was finishing my manicure when the door banged open. An older woman came in holding a younger woman upright, and nodded brightly to Tony. "This is Mrs. Adams," she said.

For all her youth, Mrs. Adams' face was pale in that ashy tone of the very ill. She moved awkwardly as the older woman led her to Tony's chair. "Mrs. Adams needs her hair restyled. Give her a cute pixie cut. You would like that, wouldn't you dear?" And without waiting for an answer, the older woman motioned to Tony to go ahead. "The plane leaves at five," she went on, her voice stridently gay. "While you have your wash and set, and oh yes, a manicure, I will pick up your luggage and be right back." She chattered on about the beauty of Puerto Rico, how much fun Mrs. Adams would have there, how tan she would get, and how darling she would look in her new clothes. Then she sidled toward us. "Her son died you know. Only child—eight years old. He is being cremated today, right now in fact. She is going on a vacation with her husband; he is also a mess about it. While they are gone, I am moving her into a new apartment. I am keeping her very busy today so she won't think of the cremation. Watch her now, she must not break down." She sidled back to the silent figure, but I could tell that Tony had heard what she had told us because his face was flushed.

The older woman continued talking and laughing for a few more minutes and finally left with a wave. "Be back soon and off you will go, dear. You will just love Puerto Rico . . ."

Mrs. Adams remained silent, gazing into the mirror with a blank stare, and then as we watched, tears began to drop down her cheeks almost in rhythm with the snip of the scissors. Adrianna jumped toward her, but Tony waved her away.

"My little boy's eyes are so blue," Mrs. Adams said in a husky voice. "It was just a sore throat. My husband is with him now. They are cremating—no—no—" and she screamed one long scream. Tony leaned over and yelled, "Cry, that's it, go on, cry!" He put his arms around her and half carried her to the back of the shop, motioning Adrianna to follow. They were gone a long time. When he reappeared, he was nodding. "She is still crying. Adrianna is holding her like she is one of our kids. What is the sense of pretending she is going on a vacation—new clothes—new apartment? That stupid woman!" He shrugged and rolled his eyes, looking like a prophet out of the Old Testament. "Someone we love dies. Okay, we cry. We cry for weeks. We suffer. But we face it. Damn it, we face it, otherwise—. Listen, they will be lucky if this little woman does not kill herself on this—this vacation!"

I had watched the scene with horror, remembering

what a psychologist had told me, "All too often a patient comes to me with one problem only to discover
that his real problem is an unresolved grief of five, ten,
or even fifteen years standing which has eroded his
whole life since."

This is an extreme example of the errors in judgment friends can make. But let us be charitable. That
older woman was sincere. She really believed it was
possible to avoid grief. Most of us are not as flagrant in
our mistakes, and at best it is not easy to decide "how
to help" because there is grief and grief, and the measuring of its intensity is like measuring one snowflake
against another.

Right after my husband's funeral, my two sons and
I were alone in my apartment for a short time. As
my younger son, Peter, opened the hall closet to put
my coat away, I caught sight of my husband's topcoat
and my control snapped. "Oh, God," I cried, "I will
never make it without him—never." I ran toward my
bedroom, but I could hear Peter say: "I cannot bear
to see her like this. I just cannot bear it!"

"I know," Bob said. "What can we do—what can
we say?" and his voice was like an echo of my own
despair. I swerved and walked back to my sons. Their
faces were drawn with sorrow, their eyes dull with
fatigue.

These very young men had shared every moment
of the horror of watching their father die. They had
helped me select the clothes to be sent to the chapel,

arrange the funeral, talk with family and friends. And I was about to run away from them to cry alone. It was senseless. Trapped in my own desolation, I had forgotten they were in grief, too. They had just lost their father.

"You have been wonderful," I said. "Don't stop now. Understand I need to cry—I must." They both nodded.

It is at such times that a good friend, who is empathetic and quietly there, is of such value to a grieving family.

So it goes; you as a friend can hinder recovery, but the converse is true. You as a friend can help—really help.

The griever may not know it, but now you do. At this point you and he are not equals; he is like a lost child, and you are like a loving parent. You reach out to find him. You take the initiative. You show the affection, the warmth. For he is faced with the unspeakable agony of admitting the loved one is dead, never to return; the mountainous task of adjusting to a new way of life; the tortuous effort to overcome an all-pervading apathy.

Now what is your role? The initiative is still yours. You call him. Invite him for a walk, to your place for dinner—small distractions at first. If he refuses five times, do not give up or insist, just keep asking in a casual way: "It's a nice day, let's have lunch. I can call for you about twelve." And continue to phone, visit, and suggest things to do together, and always listen. If he asks for advice, and only if he asks, tell him what you think, but do not try to sell your ideas to him— just offer them. Find out what he is doing with those endless weekends and holidays, and remember the loneliest time of the day is at twilight, a good hour to see him if you can.

All the professionals agreed that a widow's role is the most difficult. It is so easy to relegate her to daytime activity. What about the long empty evenings? As time passes, she will begin to need male companionship, and it is up to you to find available men. Easy enough to say that you do not know any. Ask around, someone you know may have an available uncle, nephew, cousin, friend, or business associate. Don't you decide whom she would like or dislike—let her make her own decisions. Introduce her to any and every available man. And here is where an old saw really works: "If at first you don't succeed, try, try again!" It is not up to her family or her friends to guide her back into feeling like a female—it is up to you!

The widower's problems are different. Statistically there are eight widows for every widower. He will be besieged by invitations—but he will need help in the mundane areas of his life. The myriad details of running a household—the meals, the laundry, et cetera. And he, too, faces loneliness, guilt, and fear of the future. Although he is never the social liability the widow is, he needs to feel his friends believe in him, need him, and are available.

As a friend it is not your role to manipulate or cajole; your primary role through the spiraling stages of grief, no matter how they vary, is to be available, understanding, and above all a good listener. Shakespeare said: ". . . the grief that does not speak/Whispers the o'erfraught heart and bids it break."

You might be bewildered by a griever who seems to be doing well, going out, meeting new people, then suddenly collapses; but the three stages of grief overlap erratically. Someone in shock can suffer; someone suffering can show healthy signs of recovery; someone who seemed to accept a death with equanimity may regress into shock without warning; someone who pushed himself into great social activity too soon may break down months later. Many a griever makes mistakes in judgment because he really believes he is thinking clearly, when in truth he is acting out of panic. Thus he forces himself to make decisions before he is capable of any decision at all.

Since intense grief can disfigure the finest mind, your time and your active concern are the two most precious gifts you can offer. For given these, man has the courage to reshape his own life—creatively.

Chapter Eight

HOW TO HELP YOURSELF

HOPEFULLY you have come to a point in your grief where you yearn to help yourself, but feel unsure of how to proceed. It is a valid dilemma, for, more often than not, grief has destroyed your self-image and sorrow has brought you a lassitude that saps your energy. You are like a pilot "flying blind," and the way ahead is fogged-in with a density of frightening clouds.

You need to charter a new course. Learn in which direction you would like to go, what you want.

I remember a widower saying: "I don't know what I want." That statement was only a half truth. He didn't want to make the effort. It seemed easier to live in darkness than to crawl toward the light. "A whole new life," he told himself, "it's too big to contemplate." He had forgotten that there are small steps toward narrower horizons; that living each day is enough. Thus a mental outlook can be reversed by self-discipline and redirection. One day at a time—one goal for each day.

As a griever you are vulnerable, easily hurt, very sensitive. But if you hoard feelings of disappointment; if you cringe at every slight; if you allow bitterness or cynicism to color your thinking, you will alienate the sympathetic, understanding people along with the insensitive.

All grievers of all ages need guidance. In my own case, professional advice seemed wise. I consulted a hypnotist. He believed that an "escape motivation" only delays recovery and that hypnotism is not for grievers. Therefore he asked many questions before he agreed to talk with me. Finally satisfied that I had lived through my shock and suffering and was ready to digest his suggestions, he showed me a simple kind of self-help, not hypnotism, which was in essence a method of redirecting thoughts and behavior—a method for all grievers except the very very young.

He motioned me toward a big easy chair, asked me to breathe slowly and deeply, to relax one muscle after another until I felt as limp as a rag doll. Then he asked me to picture a happy scene. But every scene that came to mind included my husband. "That's my problem," I said. "I see no happiness without him."

"All right," he said. "Concentrate on a blank white wall. Can you do that? Good." And it *was* good. "Now picture yourself doing something you've never done before."

"I've never traveled alone," I said.

"Picture yourself in an airplane. Watch it soar into the sky. See yourself in the plane, relaxed and smiling. See the soft clouds, the sunlight."

Again it was good. He said: "A human being can concentrate on only one thought at a time. Suggest this to all grievers: Every morning breathe deeply and slowly; relax every muscle; picture a blank wall and then against that blank wall picture what you expect to do that day. See yourself doing it with ease, interest, and in good humor."

This first step in redirecting your thoughts is very difficult. I tried his theory but drifted away from the necessary discipline of it, again and again; distracted by memories of happier days when life held so much promise; torn by an overpowering fear that now I had no future at all. But each time I forced myself to practice his method, the day went very well indeed.

It sounds ridiculously simple, hardly worth trying. And yet, no matter for whom you grieve, with a measure of perseverance it can be a most effective first step. In a way, that blank white wall is symbolic of erasing the past and providing a clean slate. And when you imagine yourself facing the day in an ideal frame of mind, it is like laying out a pattern of behavior to follow.

Laughingly I called it building castles in the air, but I knew it was one way to learn to concentrate again.

The value of concentration for all grievers yields unexpected dividends in remolding a self-image. Every griever has so many decisions to make, and it is all too tempting to allow oneself to be told what to do. My mistakes were big and small. For one small example: My husband and I owned a co-op apartment at the beach. After he died, I dreaded going back there, but my neighbors persuaded me. "You won't be alone," they said. "We are all your friends."

Thus reassured, relying on their words, I moved to that little apartment which my husband and I had so enjoyed. True, during the day I was not alone, but as the day cooled into twilight, my friends disappeared into their own apartments and I was very much alone —to cook a lonely meal and face the endless hours until sleep, the reluctant rescuer, blacked out TIME.

Were these cruel people? No, just unaware that grief is so enervating there is little room left for creative solitude.

Every big or small decision is a mental exercise, a challenge. You can learn to analyze every bit of advice and where it would lead you. Not from another person's perspective, but from your own. You can learn that solitude is vital to inner restoration; a time to face what you are and what you want to be; to accept the fact that you are still a human being with present responsibilities, past experiences, and future hopes.

And while you are concentrating, THINK: How do you want to look? Surely, interested, neat, and attractive. Against that blank white wall you picture each day, see yourself standing there—how would you like to look? Now go to your mirror. Try to fuse the image with reality. Has tragedy tightened the lines around your mouth—slackened your posture? It costs nothing except will power to smile and think tall. Now let the pendulum swing between activity and rest, between the work of self-improvement and a quiet evaluation of that work, between friendly involvement with others and solitude.

This division of time keeps you from becoming a "loner," which is important, since you cannot grow just by looking within yourself, nor can you grow by listening and accepting every idea from others. Then as you study yourself and concentrate on self-improvement, it is almost inevitable you will find aspects of your character and personality you would like to change.

If you do not expect too much of yourself too soon, and are patient with mistakes you make along the way, you have entered a challenging new world.

I thought I had better talk with a plastic surgeon. Some grievers want to change their appearance. He said, "I'm often asked to operate on men as well as women. If their grief is fresh, I will not touch them. Plastic surgery cannot alleviate grief, nor is it a substitute for sorrow. No. It's a waste of my time and their money. I advise them to see me again in a year or so. Even then, I am always careful to accept only those patients whose looks will improve appreciably from cosmetic surgery."

Once you have started to redirect your mental outlook, improve your physical appearance, decide on a brighter personality, forgive yourself many of the guilty memories, seek solitude for self-understanding and self-improvement; you will find you want to share these changes with others.

"But how do you make new friends?" a griever asked, who was alone in a strange city.

Again I asked for professional advice. A social worker. "Concern for others is the healthiest antidote to loneliness," he said. "Practice on everyone you meet —your co-workers, the elevator man, the delivery boy. Friendly greetings, warm smiles, a willingness to listen. And when you have the opportunity to talk with someone you would like for a friend, watch your conversation. Don't be afraid to speak of an experience which has been deeply significant to you or express an honest opinion. If he disagrees, don't 'sell' your idea. He'll be interested if you have been genuine rather than one who spouts generalities or brags about what he has, what he does, or who he knows. Those are dull subjects. Better to listen than to bore; better to offer thoughtful personal ideas of your own than to quote someone else. And the worst bores of all are those who monopolize any conversation. The compulsive talker may be amusing but he is also tiring. Good conversation is open communication. Only a lecturer holds the floor alone, and all too often makes us yawn."

Despite your outward self-improvement, your emotional life may take longer to stabilize. You need friends, your work, and perhaps a hobby to feed your emotional ego. Once ready to join the world again, you cannot afford the luxury of being dour and withdrawn, waiting for others to take the initiative. If you want people to be interested in you, you have to be interesting. Interesting people know what is going on in the world. They are curious, adventurous, and friendly. They remember *your* name and *your* interests, and they usually have a special interest of their own, either in a hobby or in the interesting facets of their careers.

One of my personal problems had to do with my work. I had been a free-lance writer for years, which meant I worked at home—alone. As a widow I found it too lonely. Where could I get advice about a new and different career? I decided to talk to a vocational counselor. I recommend it to anyone, male or female, floundering about what to do or unhappy in his present occupation. She said: "It seems wasteful to throw away all your experience as a writer. Why not teach writing to others?"

"I don't know how to teach," I said.

"You can try. There's a community center nearby offering many courses. Perhaps they'd give you a chance."

They did. I discovered that for me teaching was fascinating work. An extra dividend was the friends I found in my classes.

But if you already have a career and need a hobby for those empty hours, there are inexpensive classes offered—not only in schools, but in churches, community centers, etc. If you would prefer it, volunteer workers are in constant demand, in hospitals, in political organizations, in too many places to mention. One young man and his wife spend their Saturdays at a foundling home; another grieving man, who lost wife and children in a fire, now chauffeurs the crippled and disabled to their jobs or to doctors; a woman whose son died of leukemia is a weekend volunteer at a clinic. Whether learning a hobby or doing volunteer work, you will be meeting new friends. Or perhaps you yearn to continue your long-neglected education? For a man or woman, young or old, there are night schools and extension courses available for you. Again, new places—new faces.

It is healthy to build new friendships and increase their number, but there is danger in relying on any one friend too much as an escape from loneliness or as a substitute for a lost loved one. Grief has shown you that the most intimate ties can be broken. Surely it must follow that friends cannot be your anchor to life. You are your own anchor. And though the need for relatedness with others is healthy and basic, it is courting heartache to expect too much from them, especially if you are a widow or widower. You, as a widow or widower, are wise to expect only a catch-as-catch-can relationship with others. Your interest and love is offered on a different level, the base of your life no longer shared, the belonging to that someone no longer possible, the investment and involvement with your mate no longer a reality. Face up to it: sometimes for a while, sometimes for as long as you live, you will live alone, you will be alone a great deal of the time, you will yearn to confide in someone who really cares—but who? Surely you cannot depend on any one person. You will come home to an empty house, eat alone, sleep alone, you will plan each day alone . . . alone . . . alone . . .

How easy to retreat into self-pity, resist all invitations, insist there is nothing you really want to do. Well, just remember every widow and widower fights that same battle at one time or another. It does not matter if you are young or old, if you have children or not, if you have an army of friends or a few, if you have a profession, a job or do nothing much. There are steps of apathy to overcome, there are adjustments beyond belief. And yet each griever must face it alone, suffer it alone, come out of it alone, and reclaim his life alone.

Many people have the false notion that facing such truths will make you ill. But just as crying is a healthy release of emotion, facing up to your situation, bleak as it may be, spurs you into action sooner. And action by yourself for yourself is a healthy motivation which lifts you away from despair toward a new life.

Carl Sandburg ended one of his poems with a great philosophy for all grievers. He wrote: "Be what you wish to be."

"Hah! that's ridiculous," said one widow. "I want to get married, and believe me, wishing won't make it so. I haven't met anyone. I'm sick of being with other widows. I'm sick of my married friends who invite me out to dinner—the extra woman. I'm sick of my work. I need a husband and I don't know how to find one. Some of the widows I know go out, but do they introduce me to a man they don't even like particularly? No. They just brag about their dates. I'm not aggressive, and I have some pride. I can't beg to be introduced. What will I do?"

"I don't know," I said. "Small comfort to tell you most widows are in the same boat. You don't have to meet lots of men—you just need one. Perhaps the best advice is to be ready. How you look, how you feel, what you say, what you're doing with your life—all these prepare you for that one man."

There is a very fine line between what you think you want and what you are ready to handle. Recovery cannot be rushed. A slow, painstaking growth pays the highest dividends. No griever should be pressured, or pressure himself, into any decision.

You and only you know what you think, what you want, what you want to try—your strengths and your weaknesses. You and only you know what kind of person you yearn to be, what kind of life you yearn to live, what you need to try that you have never tried before, what you need to do that you have never done before. You and only you can grope for your un-touched talents and your hidden potential and give them room to grow.

"I hate myself," a young girl who had lost her parents said: "How can I build on that? I haven't any talents and I haven't any money. I'm not pretty. What good will it do for me to picture myself successful or interesting?"

Together we went to consult a psychologist. "What you are saying is that, unless you can be pretty, success-ful, and interesting, you are nothing." He shook his head. "Let's take them one by one. You can be inter-esting, anyone can. You can find a job, or prepare to find one. Anyone can do that, too. Which leaves—can you be 'pretty'? You are a large-boned girl, you are tall. What if you got yourself a job, saved some money, had your front teeth capped—then you would be pretty. The key to recovery has only three letters: TRY."

He leaned forward, talking to her as if I were not there. "You said you hated yourself. Don't you know that hatred hardens your expression? As a matter of fact, you don't really hate yourself at all, you are angry that life threw you a low curve—and it hurts." He turned to me. "I like what the hypnotist advised. A blank white wall and picturing yourself doing and being what you'd like to do and be, but the goals must be within reason. The work on yourself must be realistic. Little use for a short, balding man to picture himself anything but a short, balding man."

"Of course," I replied. "But he could picture himself thinner if he's too heavy, friendly if he's gruff, playing the guitar if he's always dreamed of doing so. And then get going on what he wants to change."

"Ah—good. It's using the raw material of what you are and working within a realistic limit."

By now my young friend who "hated herself" was relaxed and smiling. "I've been bitter and lazy," she said.

You can change your thinking, improve your appearance, widen your social horizons, enjoy a new hobby, find satisfaction in work well done, learn a trade if need be, and begin to live again—sometimes a far wiser, stronger, and even kinder person than you ever were before.

But as you move up from grief, be prepared for setbacks. Don't be ashamed of the scar left by suffering. Don't be afraid of recurring flashes of grief.

You will be haunted by memories. The first time a widower was on a ship after his wife died, he stood alone, surrounded by excited, happy tourists. He stared into space, but he saw only the blue sky and below it the mystery of a churning sea. He remembered his honeymoon trip on a ship to Bermuda. "My darling, my darling," he whispered to an empty world. Yes, grief haunts you, reminds you, scars you, and you ask, "Why?"—but there is no answer.

No matter for whom you grieve, there are times when your heart will tighten as nostalgia swoops in and tosses you, if only for a moment, into the past. It is normal, and to be expected.

So many of my suggestions may seem too simple. "Oh, I know that," you may say, or "I always do that." Do you really know—do you always do that? Let me tell you what happened last week. I was at home correcting papers. A new widower in his late sixties, a neighbor, called on the phone. "My mother just had a stroke," he said. "Don't stay alone," I begged. "Please come over here." But the widower refused. "I'm all right," he said. "After all, my mother is eighty-six. The people in the nursing home are wonderful to her, and I want to call my sons and tell them about my mother in a little while."

I went back to correcting papers but I felt uneasy. Suddenly, I jumped away from my preoccupation with my own life and ran to the phone. I had made a stupid mistake. I called the widower. "I want to see you," I said. "Please, may I come over?"

"Oh, yes," he said eagerly.

I knew his grief was as much for his wife as for his aged mother. I had asked the wrong question. There is a world of difference between "Come to my place" and "May I come to you?" I corrected my error, but it reminded me that it is only fair to be patient with your relatives and friends. They are preoccupied much of the time with their own problems, just as I was preoccupied with correcting papers and for the moment reacted as if this troubled widower had the initiative to move toward me, when, in truth, he needed me to move toward him.

As a griever, you have the time-consuming task of ironing out your own problems, little time to criticize other people's shortcomings. Recognize them, sure. Encourage those with whom you have interests in common, but practice being diplomatic with those who prove to be superficial. Does that sound dishonest? Perhaps it is not a precise virtue. But a griever's main job is to rejoin the mainstream of life. In so doing he cannot possibly love or be loved by everyone, nor can he close his eyes to those who profess friendship and offer far less. At that point he has a choice: he can break the relationship, or he can tell himself: "I thought we were close friends. Obviously we are not. Okay, I'll accept him for what he is."

Why not, if there is some area of compatibility?

Basic and simple are the ways to help others and yourself, but who has the time to understand simple truths in this complex, high-pressure society? And yet, using these simple truths is most effective for the griever in helping himself and for those who want to help him.

The woman left alone with small children needs one kind of reorientation, the man left alone with small children another. They are confronted with the problems of juggling careers, parent substitutes, finances, and social adjustments. But everyone in grief has practical problems needing specific answers. That is why a griever seeks personal as well as professional advice. Perhaps a doctor to explain the bodily reactions to emotional shock; a lawyer to sift the practical from the impractical; an accountant to mathematize a financial position; a vocational counselor to suggest career changes or possibilities; a minister or psychologist for spiritual or emotional guidance; and close relatives and good friends to lend moral support.

Here in this book, the emphasis is not on specific situations but, rather, on recovering from the emotional trauma of grief and the inner turmoil that confuses the griever, rendering him helpless to function in his own milieu.

In our society there has been too much emphasis on what you, as a griever, "should do," and too little emphasis on what you feel and why. Grief is neither mysterious nor mystical. It is a logical pattern of reactions to a loss that is final and without hope of reprieve. Once accepted as such, you can feel free to function with a clearer understanding of yourself and how you want to reconstruct your life.

To help yourself takes time and the courage to face the truth without flinching. Little use to pick up the pieces of what you were and try to patch them together. What you were is history. Yesterday is over;

let it linger, for it will anyway, to enhance and deepen the dimensions of your character—but concentrate on today.

Help yourself. You can do it far better than anyone else.

Chapter Nine

HOW MINISTERS HELP

Many grievers turn to their ministers for help in bereavement and for the solace and spiritual comfort which they offer. One young man, whose best friend collapsed and died in his arms from a heart attack, said to me: "I have noticed that people with faith meet grief better than those of us who do not have such faith. I wish I knew why."

We have invited six ministers of different faiths and traditions to tell you in their own words how they try to help those in grief.

The Rev. Leon M. Flanders, pastor
First Presbyterian Church, Greenlawn, New York

As a Christian pastor, I find that the ministry to those who grieve is one of the most challenging and

fulfilling of all the ministries I perform. In the first
stage of shock there is little that can be done to alleviate grief except to comfort and assure. My first endeavor is to establish an empathy with those who
grieve and to encourage a release of emotion. In most
instances, some consideration must be given to funeral
arrangements. This leads naturally to a discussion of
the one for whom the grief is being expressed. I try
to see the deceased through the eyes of the ones I am
seeking to comfort, so that my later ministries to them
may be as personalized and meaningful as possible. I
always end my first visit to a grieving family with a
very brief prayer in which I commend them, as well
as their loved one, to the love and mercy of God.

During the next several days I may call once or
twice upon a person or family before the funeral service is held, depending on what I sense to be their needs.
In some instances practical help may be required, in
which case I turn to people in my congregation whom
I know to be willing to assist. Naturally, I can provide a much more comprehensive ministry to members
of my own congregation than I can to strangers.

During the period when suffering is most intense,
I lean heavily upon Scripture, drawing freely upon
the great and wonderful promises of God to remember
us in our suffering and to comfort us in our grief. If I
find areas of experience equivalent to some I have
known, I share mine with those I am trying to comfort.
For example, my mother died of cancer when I was

in my early twenties. I can share with young people similarly afflicted the new dimension of faith into which this loss brought me—how God became very real to me at that time in terms of His presence and the comfort and strength I derived from Him. Invariably, I sense a lift of the spirit and a renewed hope on the part of those who are grieving.

After the funeral I endeavor to offer counsel concerning adjustments which may have to be made. I also try to ascertain if the one bereft has a supporting faith strong enough to see him through this period of return to normal living. Here, again, what I can do depends very much upon my personal relationship, whether the person is a member of my congregation or not.

Where the bereaved are from outside and I have had no prior relationship, I still try to provide counsel or any other kind of ministry, as I sense a need for, and a willingness to receive it.

I always try to assure those who grieve, no matter how deeply, that their grief can be assuaged and, if given the opportunity, completely overcome. Time, of course, and reinvolvement in normal patterns of living help in this direction.

Some people feel that the measure and length of their grief is an index to the depth of their love for someone they have lost. Just recently a young man came to me who had been involved with a friend in a tragic accident. The friend had lost his life. The young man told me of the deep attachment that had bound himself and his friend together. He now wanted to know why he did not continue to grieve more deeply over his loss. "I find I am able to involve myself in my usual activities and enjoy them," he said.

"Do you miss your friend?" I asked. His face took on a bleak expression for a moment.

"Oh yes," he answered, "I miss him so much!"

He was grieving but he didn't know it. This is healthy grief. It is grief that is without guilt, grief that is not self-centered. He had accepted his grief in a mature, constructive way.

Grief stems from love and all its kindred emotions. It is felt by the young as well as the old. It should be accepted and expressed. But, most of all, it should be subjected to the spiritual therapies which God has provided for its cure as well as assuaged by the comfort and help we give one another in time of sorrow.

JOSEPH G. KEEGAN, S.J., PH.D.
Associate Professor of Psychology, Staff Psychologist, Counseling Center, Fordham University, Bronx, New York

The pastoral counselor can be true to his religious responsibility toward those under his charge only if he is prepared to treat them as total, unique persons. And it is as existential persons that they experience such debilitating emotional states as conflict, anxiety, guilt, and grief—this last being the focus of our present interest.

Clergymen of all denominations have Old and New Testament witness to the inevitability of their presence to suffering. For the priest-counselor who is a Catholic, the challenge of grief should be a suitable stimulus to revise what has unfortunately been a tendency so to stress values in the hereafter as to discourage the exploration of better ways of fostering happiness in the present life.

Who are the people of God who are beset with grief and yearn for the solace and comfort which in many cases only the pastoral counselor can offer? The sick. The bereaved husband or wife. A family facing divorce or separation. The family into which a maimed or retarded child may have been born. The list could be continued to include the personal and familial aftermath of serious accidents that are near catastrophic and impending calamities such as loss of employment, poverty, or the diagnosis of cancer. All have in common some manifestation of that syndrome which we designate as grief.

We are not by any means in possession of a fully scientific account of the complete course of the grief syndrome. But a few careful studies of the aftermath of what happened to people in Hiroshima or to passengers on the *Andrea Doria* may serve as a paradigm concerning the effects of disaster in the human psyche. There are generally three stages, of which the first (called shock) shows itself as a state of stupefaction. People appear stunned as though sedated and without direction. While they are in this stage, nothing can be done by way of positive intervention or constructive communication, but the clergyman should be aware of the value of his presence and the likely assistance of that silent communication to be found in his empathy.

Following shock there is a period of recoil during which the afflicted person reacts with strong emotion, perhaps showing unusual anger and hostility or, conversely, such inappropriate behavior as giggling and silliness. It is at this stage that psychological intervention is most useful and necessary, and the priest or minister must carefully assess his role and the skills he has to meet the situation. It would be during this phase, I should think, that he might heed the caution about possible referral—or, more usually, seek assurance from a professional that he is clear about the proper goals of treatment and the required extent of intervention.

The third or final stage in grief is designated as "recall" and is calculated to lead toward recovery. This may be described as a phase of tensive restlessness in which there is some manifestation of preoccupation with memories of the traumatic experience. This is essentially a healthy reaction, and the pastoral counselor can be of tremendous assistance in helping his counselee accept a realistic appraisal of the significance of the traumatic experience and a feasible mode of reconstructing his or her life in accord with a revised perspective. It is clear that the entire process is likely to be a long and complex interaction between the helping counselor and the person needing help. The counselor must, therefore, be convinced that he is probably the only person capable of providing an integrated intervention that will combine the pertinent elements of spiritual, religious values and psychological understandings in his ministry.

Instead of prescribing lofty but abstract formulae, his ministry can become a dynamic encounter in which his love and feeling for people will produce dialogue in which God's love is better reflected and spiritual values are seen in a meaningful context.

THE REV. T. CARLETON LEE, RECTOR
St. John's Episcopal Church, Cold Spring Harbor, New York

In all the deepest human experiences, whether they be welcome or devastating, the fundamental and obvious rule in pastoral care is to focus attention on the person and not on matters of doctrine. The tendency of many clergy, particularly in their younger, inexperienced days, is to look upon a crisis event in a person's life as an opportunity to teach religion. This tendency inculcates a desire to use spiritual authority to order a person's reactions and general behavior according to a set pattern supposedly evidencing "faith" or a more specific religious commitment. Many people, in the uncertainty of forming reactions to deeply felt events, are greatly influenced by such direction, but in the long run it turns out to be a blind alley emotionally for them.

Grief and bereavement are, of course, the most devastating experiences in the whole range of pastoral care, particularly if they occur suddenly. The initial reaction of shock leaves many people disoriented and looking for guidance. The imprint of cultural patterns learned primarily in the family is usually very strong. Oftentimes the influence of the immediate social group to which the person belongs is also of great importance, sometimes dangerously so. But in the long run, the most important factor will be the individual's own personality and character, and encouragement which is supportive and strengthening. In other words, the pastor will be increasing the burden and complicating the situation if he tries to convey to the grief-stricken person the idea that religious faith demands certain feelings or outward behavior. Should he attempt this approach, the griever will unwittingly be falling in line with all the other forms of social and cultural compulsion that make the working out of grief difficult.

As an instance, let me describe a current form of social compulsion which I regard with great apprehension. One's friends encourage in every way the immediate return to "normalcy," and particularly in respect to social occasions. Such advice implies that grief can be by-passed, that "there is no death," and that bereavement should be allowed to make only a casual ripple on the course of one's life. Behind such advice there is, moreover, both a reaction to excessive displays of grief and mourning, and the quite valid psychological principle that activity, routine, and the resumption of normal relationships have their therapeutic value. But in its worst form, this social attitude encourages the running away from reality on the part of both the person bereaved and the group whose support and compassion he most needs. Should the pastor encourage this pattern of response by giving it a religious label ("Everything is all right, he is living in heaven with God"), he is reversing the function of the pastoral relationship, which is to strengthen and support the bereaved person, and thus help him to deal with reality— and bereavement by death is a stern example of life's realities.

What, then, should the pastor say and do? In the initial period of shock, he must encourage the individual to use whatever emotional outlets are available. If it is weeping, then there should be weeping; if talking in great detail about the circumstances of the death, then there must be a sympathetic listener; if it is to express all the pent-up resentments of the previous relationship, then there must be nonjudgmental understanding. In public, certain cultural traditions expect the stiff-upper-lip, and it is often important that the grief-stricken person conform to this for his own self-respect; but in the family or in private, there has to be some purgative outlet. At a later time, usually, the pastor can offer the help that comes from religious belief by discussing the awful existential theological problems that arise out of grief, in the form of the question, "Why?" or in a deepening awareness of the basic ambiguities of all life. Finally, there must be constant reassurance that the unusual emotional experiences accompanying grief are in most cases not abnormal or "crazy," but an important part of the process of reconstitution. And ultimately, the fact must be faced that grief is never fully resolved, that the hole in life is never filled up again, and that there is a permanent pain of loneliness, which is remembrance's somber and valuable witness to life.

THE REV. CLAYTON Z. MILLER, PASTOR
Union Methodist Church, East Northport, New York

I discover there are two large categories into which the griever falls: either a category of shock because of the suddenness of the death or a category of loss mixed with relief that comes after a prolonged illness.

In the case where there has been a long-term illness, there is often a sense of guilt because of the feeling of relief and release that they sometimes feel is inappropriate. To be able to draw out this grief and to dispel it is often a primary concern of mine. Such a griever usually finds recovery more quickly than those in shock situations, but he also needs great support through his suffering, which is often greater than he anticipated it would be.

Where the death has been a sudden and shocking experience, the first few days are very confused and the person is not receptive to any direct counseling but only to the pastor's presence and whatever comfort he can bring by use of the Scriptures and traditional services. However, a week or so later his receptivity to counseling is evidenced by many questions and the expressions of many kinds of emotions and feelings. It is my practice to counsel such persons on a very regular basis, sometimes even by appointment so that they know when I am coming and have an opportunity to think of questions they want to ask and feelings they want to express.

To give an example: A ten-year-old boy was hit by a car while riding his bicycle. He lay in a coma for eight days. The doctors gave little hope to the parents, indicating that if he should live there was such brain damage that he would not be normal. The parents kept constant vigil at his bedside those eight days, neglecting home, four other children, work. When the boy passed away on the eighth day, the parents felt that the first demand for their time was the other four children. There was no wake at the funeral home; there was no viewing of the boy. There was a memorial service in the church, which the parents indicated was to be a service that would affirm the faith which was the basis of their hope. In this particular instance, as I called on the parents at the hospital each day, they had the opportunity to go through the early stages of shock and when the actual death occurred, there was already the beginning of recovery. Of course, the stage of suffering was still to be endured, but when there is so much else to live for (the four children), recovery comes more quickly.

MORRIS SHAPIRO, RABBI
South Huntington Jewish Center, Huntington Station, New York

Theoretically speaking, the time to develop a mature philosophy toward death is before, not after, it strikes, just as one should learn to swim before one is shipwrecked, not after.

When Rabbi Bunam lay dying, his wife burst into tears. He said, "What are you crying for? My whole life was only that I might learn how to die."

Judaism does not permit a morbid preoccupation with death. The Jewish identity is with life. Death is recognized as an inevitable concomitant of G-d's divine plan for His creatures. Therefore death should be anticipated without horror, but with abiding faith in the goodness, the love, and mercy of G-d.

Commenting on the verse from Psalms, "I shall not die, but live," Rabbi Yatzhak said: "In order really to live, a man must give himself to death. But when he has done so he discovers that he is not to die—but to live."

However, while we acknowledge the inevitability and significance of death, the death of a dear one is often a deeply disturbing emotional experience. The average man is rarely, if ever, quite prepared for it. And as a rabbi who is called to minister to people during their bereavement, I rely on the teachings and techniques that Judaism has developed to meet the challenge of death.

We do not attempt to "comfort the bereaved while the deceased lies before him." We do not encroach upon the privacy demanded by fresh bereavement. We try to help the individual to live through the pain and distress by prescribing a round of ceremonies to be performed by the bereaved, which allows him openly to express his grief.

Once death strikes, there is a religious obligation to make certain that the departed receives a proper burial. All other religious obligations are void in the face of this act of lovingkindness. Thus, the bereaved is inevitably impressed with the first priority Judaism accords to the deceased.

After the body has been prepared for burial, the bereaved sits near the departed, reciting psalms and allowing his emotions unrestrained expression. Just before the funeral services, the *Kreah*, or tearing of the clothes of each mourner, takes place, accompanied with a prayer which affirms that G-d is a "Judge of Truth."

On the return of the bereaved from the cemetery, Jewish practice, in its intuitive wisdom, has designated a pattern of observances which diminishes in intensity as time goes on. These practices lead the mourner progressively from inconsolable grief, through resignation, and into a reaffirmation of life. The first mourning period lasts for seven days. It begins with and includes the day of burial. The first meal that the mourners eat upon return from the cemetery is provided and prepared by neighbors and friends.

The purpose of the seven-day mourning is to create an opportunity for communication between the bereaved and those who share the sorrow of his loss. A burden which is shared is lightened. Services should be held at the house of the mourners morning and evening wherever practical.

Following the initial seven-day mourning period, the remaining twenty-three days are counted as part of the thirty days following burial. It is a period during which mourners return to everyday activities, but refrain from entertainment such as television and parties. Throughout this period and until eleven months pass from the date of death, immediate relatives recite the *Kaddish* at synagogue services daily.

There is no prayer in the Hebrew liturgy that has captivated the heart and the senses of the Jewish mourner as has the *Kaddish*. In itself, the *Kaddish* is not a prayer for the dead. It speaks, rather, of faith in the ultimate establishment of G-d's rule among men, and the coming of abundant peace to the world.

Above all, the recitation of the *Kaddish* is a public proclamation that even in the face of death G-d's greatness must be recognized, and life must be affirmed. For this prayer voices our belief in that which is imperishable, and renews our faith in the eternal quality of the human spirit.

Here is a translation of part of the *Kaddish:*

> Exalted and hallowed be G-d's great name,
> In the world He created according to His will,
> May His sovereignty be revealed,
> Speedily in our lifetime,
> And the life of all mankind,
> Let us say, Amen.

The round of ceremonies allowing the individual to express his grief does not mean that the expression of grief should be unduly prolonged. The Rabbis in the Talmud, using the words of Jeremiah, insisted: "Weep ye not for the dead nor bemoan him beyond measure." To remain enslaved to the memory of one long passed becomes a form of idol worship.

These are the provisions of Jewish tradition for facing grief—a round of ceremonies, and affirmation of our faith in G-d and in the worthwhileness of life. There is no substitute for grief but grieving—but following the Jewish way of life can be of great help and solace during the period of sorrow.

RALPH STUTZMAN, MINISTER
The Unitarian Universalist Fellowship of Hunting-ton, Huntington, New York

One of the great insights that existentialists have stressed in our generation is that by facing death, your own personal death, a person gains a completely different perspective on the value of time, which is a religious category in and of itself.

Therefore, one of the main elements of my preaching and personal ministry is to aid people to confront death before it actually happens. The large majority of my fellowship's members are humanists. I know of no one who believes in personal immortality. Therefore, long before a death occurs there is a realistic view, a realistic understanding of its finality. One might think such a view would cause those close to the deceased to grieve the more because of this view. This has not been my experience.

As a result, ministering to people in a death situation is a process of honest confrontation with the fact of the deceased's death. During such a period, I emotionally hold the hands of those who are in grief. Their grief, unless it is psychologically abnormal, is legitimate and accepted as such. If the grief is abnormally prolonged or abnormal in its manifestation, I refer them to a professional therapist, a practice readily acceptable in our fellowship. But abnormal grief has happened only rarely. The death of a loved one is always, always a shock. However, emphasizing a realistic theology, a confrontation of life's demands and death's inevitability, plus a stress on emotional health in all aspects of living, I believe has aided parishioners through the crisis of death within a family.

Chapter Ten

UP FROM GRIEF

Throughout these chapters you have met all kinds of grievers from a wide spectrum of social, economic, and ethnic backgrounds. Among them you have met a princess and a well-known TV personality, a dressmaker and an eminent stockbroker, a carpenter, a policeman, a socialite, a refugee from Hitler's Germany, and a Boston schoolteacher. And more, many more. What does it matter? Grief and its anxieties have made them as one. Fear has shadowed their self-confidence. Some have used that fear as a challenge, rising above it—as a hero on the field of battle does—to fight their way back from the aloneness of grief into the mainstream of life.

Those who came up from grief were afraid, but not too afraid to try for recovery. Those who succeeded in creating a new life did so by accepting the loss of a loved one and its aftermath of shock and suffering with the philosophy: *What is, is. What I feel, I feel. What I am, I am. What I can change, I will.* Sometimes they needed help in facing their sense of guilt, self-pity, and bitterness. Sometimes they faced it themselves, knowing that life owed them nothing; that life is not tidy; that nothing worth having comes easily.

A psychoanalyst told me that grievers even in their sixties come to him, not for formal analysis but for a short period of counseling, using him as a sounding board and with the knowledge that "two heads are better than one" when you are confused and in conflict.

Is it not admirable that people well on in years can admit they are in conflict and seek help, whether it be from a social worker, a psychologist, a minister, a doctor, or a trusted friend or relative?

Sometimes the reason grievers are in conflict is because they try to conform to what is expected of them, which is in direct opposition to what they really want. Sometimes the conflict is within themselves. What they want is not acceptable to their self-image. And sometimes they are frustrated because they are misunderstood. A young woman whose fiancé was killed in the war said: "I confided to a friend that I was lonely for Chris—my fiancé. I thought she understood. But she did not. She assumed that because I was lonely, I was ready to fill the social hours with anybody rather than be alone. Not so. I still prefer to select my companions and I still prefer to divide my time between sociability and privacy. She had misinterpreted the meaning of my words. Yes, I am lonely for a man who loved me, and whom I loved—just that and no more. I try to fill the gap he left with good friends, a career in which I offer a share of love, hard work, and involvement. Perhaps someday a man will come along who is as right for me as I am for him. But at no time can that gap be filled by just 'anybody.' "

This griever's reactions are not unique. Whatever the loss, grievers are often misunderstood. I remember a mother who had lost a seven-year-old daughter, and her shocked reaction when everyone, including her doctor, advised her to have another child as soon as possible. "Of course we'll have more children if we can," she said. "But I don't feel I lost 'a child'—I lost a person. Her name was Emily. She was an individual. I loved her! Why don't they understand?"

I remember a widower whose friends decided he must "go out and have a good time." But a good time for him was not night clubs and carousing, as his friends seemed to think—it was a day in the country, a game of tennis, riding a bicycle—the outdoors.

When a griever knows what he wants, and is open to suggestions and tries new avenues of enjoyment if only to reject them, there is little conflict. The conflict arises when he loses contact with himself and forgets that the final choice of what his new life will be is—his. If it is right for him, it is right. If it is wrong for him, it is wrong.

That sounds dogmatic and omits the possibility that a griever can become confused because he is convinced that what he wants is wrong for him.

One young man believed he "should" invite his widowed mother-in-law to move in with him, his wife, and two small children. Their house was large. It was logical and he was very fond of her. "But, it's such a permanent decision," he said in talking it over with a friend. "Suppose it doesn't work out. It would be cruel to tell her to leave!"

His friend listened, until he had a clearer picture of the widow's financial status (which was adequate), the daughter's relationship with her mother and how the children reacted to their grandmother. There seemed to be no problem, their relationships were good. Then he said: "Why don't you ask your mother-in-law what she plans to do? If she doesn't know, why don't you write and invite her for a visit? This is June. You could ask her to come for the month of July."

The young man liked the idea. He found his mother-in-law had no specific plans. He invited her for the visit. "Oh! I'd love that," she said. She stayed three weeks. "This has been a marvelous change for me," she said, "and it has given me time to think. Now I want to get back home and see my friends, look for a job . . ."

"Whenever you feel like getting away from the city, will you visit us?" he asked, and he meant it.

"Would it be convenient for me to come over the Labor Day weekend?"

"It's a date," he said.

The young man had forgotten his mother-in-law would have ideas of her own. Once reassured that a loving family liked her company, she was ready to live her own life and plan her future.

Grievers have another perplexing question, one they often hold in secret for fear of ridicule or of answers they can neither understand nor accept. They wonder: "Where is the one who died now?" My own father believed my mother's spirit was with him always. "I know she's here," he said. "I can't explain how I know, but she's here!" A widow said she, too, was sure her husband was close by all the time, watching over her like a Guardian Angel.

Others see heaven as clearly as if they had visited there, and still others believe that when you die—you die. They deny the hereafter as if they had proof.

A philosopher said: "A person believes what he wants to believe, whatever makes him comfortable. For those who are concerned and unsure of what to believe, I suggest this: Ask yourself, What difference does it make? You may hope, even yearn, for an afterlife, but why become overly concerned about a truth, whatever it is, that you cannot know or prove, in life?"

Life for the griever is an uphill struggle, which he

can accept as necessary or condemn as impossible. The choice is his. And of all the obstacles along the way, guilt is the hardest to overcome. I'm talking about neurotic guilt as against normal guilt. A neurotic guilt is more than regret that you were not always kind, patient, and the perfect husband or wife, mother or father, daughter or son, brother or sister or friend. It is the overwrought conscience that bedevils you when you love again; or when any feeling of joy overrides sorrow; or when satisfaction in a job well done taunts you.

The neurotic guilt of a son who finds his stepmother compatible and understanding, and hates himself for "forgetting" his mother. Or the daughter who encourages her father to remarry and then blames herself for an unholy alliance of desertion.

How can a griever cure a neurotic guilt? Through understanding what love for another human being really is and what it is not. It is not pure and it is not perfect, because the human being is neither pure nor perfect. We get angry at those we love, we feel hostile at times and impatient. We lash out in fury, saying and doing things we regret. But is it not true that the deeper our love, the greater its turmoil and the lustier its anger? When two human beings love each other, they are involved, and the very involvement shows a preoccupation one for the other, but they are still human beings and no love is more perfect than those who love. In truth, anger expressed can clear the air and deepen understanding. A psychiatrist said: "Some resentment and hostility between those who love is normal. I worry more about people who never exchange an angry word. They are either repressed or bored."

"I heard a teenager say he detested his father," I said. "Why was he heartbroken when his father died?"

"Still guilt," the psychiatrist said. "And ambivalence. I'd bet he loved his father as much as he detested him."

"What about grievers who felt a sense of duty rather than love?"

"If it's a true statement, their grief would be shorter than others, but if they secretly enjoyed being needed, or secretly resented the duty, the result would be guilt. You see, in each case they call it one thing and feel another. But if it were really a sense of duty and nothing more, that's real."

"How can we recover from a guilt that goes on too long?" I asked.

"Recognize that some guilt is normal in every grief," he said. "Admit you made mistakes, but at the same time realize the one who died made mistakes too, unless he was an infant or a small child. Acknowledge that you are not perfect, never will be. And think of what the one who died would want you to do now. Enjoy life? Learn, grow, work, love? After all, life is very short, too short to cling to the past. The individual has a responsibility to himself and to the world in which he still lives. When he comes up from grief, he moves out of the past and into the present to share his life with the living."

Let us change the supposedly cheering words "Time heals all wounds," which often frighten the griever, to "In your own time." Thus we lift ourselves away from a passive waiting to an active doing. Any situation in which you participate and have some control is always more promising and stimulating than the prospect of— waiting.

As you have seen in this book, participating in your own grief is not a complicated process. It takes courage to face facts and your real feelings. It takes patience to accept and live through shock and suffering. It takes a clear head to sift good advice from bad; to make decisions based on your very personal needs instead of what friends and relatives believe you should do. It takes self-analysis to look at yourself in the glare of truth and change what you know needs changing. It takes self-discipline to work out of shock and suffering, to rejoin the human race with dignity and a sense of your own personal worth as an individual. It takes a little common sense to plan your day so it will lead you closer to the goals you have set for your future. It takes fortitude to reach beyond your environment for new friends and still remain on easy terms with old friends. It takes imagination and will-power to present an optimistic personality to the world when your inner life is in shambles. And yet, if you have given yourself time to accept shock, time to suffer—you will be free, not of sorrow but of suppressed emotions, and ready to take one step at a time toward your unknown but provocative future.